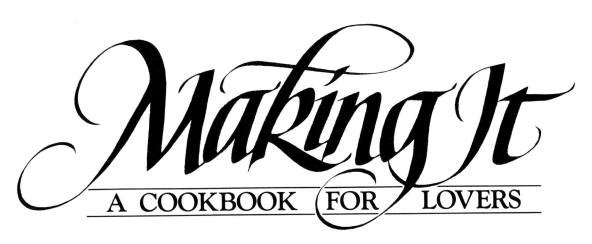

# Making It

## A COOKBOOK FOR LOVERS

Elegant and Simple Cooking for Two
as Taught by the Great Chefs (and Lovers) of Austin, Texas

*by*

LIZ R. BEREZOVYTCH

*Wishing you love alway!*
*Liz R. Berezay*

*with photographs by*
Michael Flahive

CRYSTAL CREEK PUBLICATIONS
6802 PIONEER PLACE
AUSTIN, TEXAS

For additional copies of
*Making It: A Cookbook for Lovers*
please write to:

Making It
Crystal Creek Publications
6802 Pioneer Place, Austin, Texas 78731

Please include your return address with your check
payable to Crystal Creek Publications
in the amount of $19.95 per volume, plus applicable sales tax,
plus $2.00 postage and handling, $3.50 if ordering 2 or more books.
Or, include your MasterCard or Visa number,
expiration date, and exact name on the card.

Published by
Crystal Creek Publications
6802 Pioneer Place, Austin, Texas 78731

ISBN: 0-940253-77-1

# ACKNOWLEDGMENTS

The seed of this book was planted about three years ago when I was having lunch with a dear friend of mine, Roger Makin. We were going through our wish lists of "things we'd like to do when we grow up" and lists of things that would be fun to do, when I blurted out the idea for this type of cookbook. Roger, being his usual vivacious and voracious self, began to add life to its shadowy form, and I immediately followed suit. That turned out to be one of the most entertaining lunches of the year. The idea has been through several incarnations since then, but I still must thank Roger for making the idea so indelible in my mind.

In putting the initial proposal together over a year and a half ago, there were several people who provided invaluable help and encouragement, and I would like to thank them here. They are: Lorraine Atherton, Dale Emmert, Gary Bradley, D. K. White, Keith Montgomery, Bob Emmerson, Barbara and Bob Asmussen, Michael Young, Claire Hayden, Becky Hale, Hayes Pitts, Dave Durham, Karen McCarty, my brother Frank Berezovytch, and my mother, Frances Berezovytch.

There are many people and businesses, in addition to the chefs and their spouses, who played an active roll in creating *Making It: A Cookbook for Lovers* by lending their time and effort, merchandise or homes, by making donations or concessions during the testing process, by coming up with creative solutions to problems, or by standing ready to help if and when the need arose. In no way is there any significance to the order: Lisa Sheldon, Stephanie Ferris, International Conservation Systems Inc., Richard Todd, Jim Weil, Al Adams, McMorris Ford Limousine Service, Donna Northway, Mike Reynolds, Kent Cohee, Royal Tuxedo, Frillz Forever, Peggy Crow, Debby Jenson, Melanie, Wally Pryor, Evelyn and Mel Gomez, The Emmerson Collection, Bill Brandes, Bob Robbins, Chris Collins, Dan's Liquor Store, Ken Carr, Glen Sanders, Joe McBride, McBride's Gun Shop, Mike and Roz Wilhite, Alex Martinez, Martinez Brothers Taxidermists, Arvin and Patsy Harrell, Joe Pearce, Billy Ray Hall, Hall's Wildlife Studio, Rattan Showroom, Anne Steinhauser Landscapes, Anne and Jim Hauser, Sandy Randolf, Jill Hinckley, Susan Sikora, Eve Beckwith, Mike Gentry, NASA, Kathy Sullivan, The Storehouse, Buzz Watkins, Rod Malone, The Sail & Ski Center, Pat Barrow, Solamente Mexico, Bo Albertson, Melanie Rottler, The European Influence, Nick Theodoropoulos, Reuben's Bottle Shop, Miller Uniform Company, Grady Burnette, Lissa Burnette, Bob and Susan Kay, Alexandra and John Wallace, Cathy Casey, Thomas Fleschner, Jim Adams, Larry Aiken, Bobby Earl Smith, Pat Laffey, Phil Aboussi, Pierre Bartow, Norma Gipson, Stacy Buntrock, Jess Ables, Charlie Mueller, Nan Mulvaney, Harvey Graeber, Tony Yen, Curtis Riker, Lana Riker, Vance Sack, my whole family—my uncle Norman Arlitt, my brothers Steve Berezovytch, Frank Berezovytch, and Will Berezovytch, my sister-in-law Chantal Berezovytch, my sister D Berezovytch, my mother Frances Berezovytch, and Lorraine Atherton.

Thank you all,

Liz

*DEDICATED TO THE ONES YOU LOVE,*
*HAVE LOVED, AND WILL LOVE*

# CONTENTS

# INTRODUCTION

Yes, this is a cookbook for lovers, but no, it's not a collection of aphrodisiacs. Think of it as a handbook for harried couples. In our fast-paced day of two-career couples, microwave dinners, and fast food drive-ins, we seem to be losing the art of mixing food and romance. It would be safe to say that most of us eat more often than we make love, but wouldn't it be nice to achieve the opposite, at least once in a while?

We Austinites are fortunate when it comes to mixing food and romance, because we are surrounded by a wealth of good restaurants where diners can fall in love with the food, if not with each other. In fact, eating out is a way of life for many of us in Austin. But sometimes a quiet evening at home is the best thing that two people can do for each other. And who would know better how to get things cooking at home than the people who own and run the kitchens of our favorite restaurants? When great chefs come home after a long day of preparing food for others, how do they stir up a little culinary romance for their adored? On their one day off a week, do they spend four hours sweating over a stove? Or do they rely on quick and easy dishes that can start a sweetheart simmering without turning off the cook?

In the following pages, the secrets of seventeen of the great chefs and lovers of Austin are revealed. Most of these dishes are not currently on restaurant menus, so the only way you'll get a taste is by seducing the chef or by making it with your favorite person. These tantalizing recipes are all proportioned for two (but can be doubled or tripled for gluttons or food orgies). A few of them are elaborate creations for special occasions, but in most of them the emphasis is on less time in the kitchen and more time together with the one you love. As the best cooks know, the spice of a romantic meal isn't just in the food.

Then again, maybe there is an aphrodisiac that will work for you in these pages. A quick perusal of the literature, ancient and modern, will turn up a list of alleged passion inducers as long as the menu in a Chinese restaurant, including artichokes, asparagus, banana, basil, beef, caviar, cherries, chicken, chocolate, cinnamon, crab, curry, duck, eggs, figs, garlic, ginger, grapes, green M&M's, horseradish, kidneys, lentils, liver, lobster, mint, mutton, nutmeg, onions, oysters, paprika, peas, radishes, powdered rhinoceros horn, saffron, shrimp, spinach, sugar, tarragon, thyme, tomatoes, white pepper, and yeast. Although there is no conclusive evidence that such a thing as an aphrodisiac food exists, perhaps it isn't purely coincidental that the great chefs and lovers of Austin incorporated many of those ingredients into their favorite recipes offered for this book.

Wishing you good reading, good cooking, and good loving!

# RISE AND SHINE: BREAKFASTS

Breakfast is the most important meal of the day, they say. It gets you up. It gets your juices flowing. It puts roses in your cheeks and a smile on your face. Whether it is a work day or not, you should always have a nibble in the morning.

On those busy mornings with little time to spare, you can always have a loving and fulfilling breakfast in anywhere from 5 to 35 minutes, depending on how much loving you want for breakfast and how big your appetite is. It will help if you: Get a timer for the coffee pot. Put a lock on the bedroom door if you have kids. Use instant juices. Put a toaster in the bedroom. Or put the breakfast rolls you bought from the bakery on the nightstand. A bite of a good breakfast roll, a sip of coffee or juice, a nibble on your lover's ear, a caressing hug, a promise for later, and you're off in 5 minutes. Or with a little more than a promise you're off in 35 minutes.

That's the kind of breakfast that will do on a weekday. But plan for the real thing on the weekends and holidays. That's when you can take advantage of the differences between you and your lover. For example, men usually rise faster than women. Now, that's not to say that you want to keep your man down, but you do want to keep him in bed. Suggest that he doze off for a little while and excuse yourself for a few minutes. Whip up one of these tasty breakfasts, serve it to him in bed on a decorative tray with a cup of hot coffee, the morning paper, and perhaps a Bloody Mary or a Mimosa. And slink yourself back into bed to enjoy sharing a delicious breakfast, an interesting story from the newspaper perhaps, and definitely each other.

Women, on the other hand, may enjoy a sensual and slowly savored arousal. You'll please her enormously by gently rubbing her back. Then, to whet her appetite, bring her a cup of coffee with all the cream and sugar she wants. More than likely she'll want you first. So snuggle back under the covers with her and tell her all about the wonderful things you are going to cook up for her.

Whatever your breakfast preference, you'll find it in the following recipes, from the hearty Hill Country spread to coffee with a Continental touch. You'll always be able to start your day off right with a little love and some breakfast.

# Croissants and Coffee

## Jean-Louis and Marie-Anne Dehoux

**Coffee**

                **coffee, ready to make as you usually do by
percolation or drip method**

⅛      **teaspoon cocoa powder per cup of coffee
sprinkle of salt**

**Croissants**

                **as many croissants or breakfast rolls as you think
you can eat, purchased from your local bakery**

This will work with whatever grind and strength of coffee you prefer. Just add the cocoa powder and the sprinkle of salt to the coffee before brewing. Then brew the coffee as you ordinarily would. Serve with cream and sugar as desired and your favorite croissants or breakfast rolls.

*The trick is deciding who has to get up and go to the bakery to buy the croissants. You can flip a coin, arm wrestle, or just sweet-talk your lover into picking them up the night before. The important thing is to have them in bed.*

# Migas (With Tortilla Squares) and Home Fries

### Tony Villegas

| | |
|---|---|
| 2 | large tomatoes |
| 1 | large white onion |
| 4 | fresh serrano peppers (more if you like it hot) |
| 1 | dozen thick corn tortillas |
| 4 | eggs |
| ¼ | cup liquid margarine (preferably the squeezable kind) |
| 1 | cup shredded mild cheddar or jack cheese |
| | |
| 2 | large potatoes |
| ½ | cup vegetable oil |
| | salt to taste |

## Migas

Dice the tomatoes, onion, and peppers and cut the tortillas into one-inch squares. Preheat a large skillet over medium-high heat. Beat the eggs in a bowl. Pour a small amount of margarine in the skillet, add the tomatoes, onions, peppers, and tortilla squares, and pour the remaining margarine over the mixture. Sauté for about 1 minute, then add the eggs. Sauté for another minute and add the cheese. Continue to sauté until the cheese melts and the eggs take on a soft scrambled consistency.

Timing is critical in this dish; be careful not to overcook any of the ingredients. Also, resist the temptation to stir too much, or you'll end up with bruised vegetables.

## Home Fries

Wash and dice the unpeeled potatoes. In a skillet, heat the oil on high, add the potatoes, and fry until done. Then salt to taste.

You'll be very busy for ten or fifteen minutes as you prepare these two dishes, but it is essential that they end up on the plate at the same time. To get the timing right, start the potatoes frying and then finish chopping and stirring the migas.

# Pain Perdu

*(French Toast)*
**Chef Emil**


6 to 8     thick slices of day-old French bread

### Batter

| | |
|---|---|
| 3 | eggs |
| ¼ | cup milk |
| 2 | ounces white rum |
| | dash Triple Sec |
| | dash vanilla |
| | pinch nutmeg |
| 1 | teaspoon cinnamon, in two equal parts |

### Syrup

| | |
|---|---|
| ½ | cup orange marmalade |
| ¼ | cup orange juice |
| 2 | cloves, whole |

### Garnish

| | |
|---|---|
| dollop | sour cream |
| | fruit of the season |


Stir all batter ingredients together, but use only half a teaspoon of the cinnamon. Soak half of the bread in the batter for 30 seconds and fry on a lightly greased skillet or griddle until golden brown. While the first half of the bread is cooking, stir the rest of the cinnamon into the batter. Soak the remaining slices and fry until golden brown. Remove to two plates. (Note: If you put all the cinnamon in at the beginning, the first slices of bread will absorb it all.)

Combine the syrup ingredients in a small saucepan and simmer over medium heat, stirring constantly until slightly thickened, and pour over toast.

*Pain Perdu is a good one to serve in bed, while hot, along with Mimosas or coffee. It's a delightfully refreshing wake-me-up breakfast, quick and easy to make. Almost before you've woken up, it's done and ready to start your day off right.*

# Soft-boiled Eggs With Toast Fingers

## Bobo Van Mechelen

| 1 or 2 | slices of country-style bread |
| | butter |
| 2 | eggs |
| | salt |

To soft-boil the eggs, fill a small saucepan with water (enough to completely cover the eggs) and bring to a boil over high heat. When the water is on the verge of boiling, lower the eggs one at a time into the water. Boil for 3½ minutes, then lift them out of the water and place them in egg cups.

While the eggs are boiling, toast the bread and butter it. Cut the toast into half-inch-wide strips to make the toast fingers and sprinkle with salt.

To eat, use a knife to whack off the top of the egg. (See Bobo's egg on the right.) Dip the toast fingers in the egg and put the fingers in your mouth.

*This light breakfast goes well with orange juice or Mimosas, a basket of assorted fruits, the morning paper, and a few kisses.*

# Hill Country Breakfast

## Jeff and Debby Blank

|       |                                           |
|-------|-------------------------------------------|
| 2     | six- or seven-ounce center-cut pork chops |
| 1     | tablespoon clarified butter               |
|       | salt and pepper                           |
| 2 to 4| eggs over easy or any style               |
| 2     | servings of fresh fruit in season         |
| 1     | package of biscuits from the dairy case   |

In a frying pan, melt the butter on high heat. Lightly salt and pepper both sides of the pork chops and pan fry to desired doneness. Serve with either the Fresh Herb Hollandaise (a light and tangy sauce, Debby's favorite) or Country Cream Gravy (a tried and true traditional), and over easy or your favorite style eggs.

If you want to try the hollandaise sauce, you can prepare it while the pork chops are cooking. For example, preheat the oven for the biscuits, start the pork chops, prepare the fruit next, put the biscuits in the oven to bake according to package directions, and begin the eggs and the hollandaise sauce.

If you're sticking with the Country Cream Gravy, simply put the biscuits in the oven when you start the gravy, and everything should be ready at about the same time.

Jeff's all-time favorite addition to this breakfast is Pecos cantaloupe or Ruby Red grapefruit with a splash of Triple Sec.

*The final ingredient is a patio with a view of a Hill Country sunrise.*

## Fresh Herb Hollandaise

|      |                                                       |
|------|-------------------------------------------------------|
| 6    | egg yolks at room temperature                         |
| 2    | tablespoons white wine                                |
| 1    | tablespoon lemon juice                                |
|      | dash each Tabasco, Worcestershire, salt, white pepper |
| 1½   | sticks of butter                                      |
| 1    | teaspoon chopped fresh sage                           |
| or 1 | teaspoon chopped fresh basil                          |

Put the egg yolks, wine, lemon juice, Tabasco, Worcestershire, salt, and pepper in a blender. Melt the butter and heat until bubbling. (The heat of the butter will cook the sauce, so if it is not hot enough, you may not get the best results.) Take a square of aluminum foil and push it into the blender to form a bowl into which you will pour the butter. Punch several small holes in the bottom of the bowl with an ice pick or the point of a knife. With the blender on high, slowly pour the butter into the foil. It will drain into the blending egg yolks and begin to cook the sauce. When all the butter has been added, remove the foil, add the sage or basil, blend thoroughly, and serve over the pork chops.

Hint: If the sauce is too thick, thin with a spoonful at a time of white wine. Also, other herbs of your choice, such as oregano or Mexican marigold, may be substituted for the sage and basil. And if you use dried herbs instead of fresh, remember that you'll need only half as much—in this case half a teaspoon.

## Country Cream Gravy

|     |                                                |
|-----|------------------------------------------------|
| 3   | tablespoons all-purpose flour                  |
| 1½  | cups milk (half-and-half if you like rich gravy)|
| 1   | tablespoon chicken stock or bouillon           |
|     | salt to taste                                  |
|     | fresh coarse-ground pepper to taste            |

Using the butter and oil left in the pan after you cook the pork chops, add the flour and whisk in until smooth. (Add more butter if the roux is too dry.) Brown quickly over medium-high heat. Add the milk or half-and-half while you continue to whisk the mixture until the milk is mixed through and the gravy is smooth. Add the chicken stock or bouillon, salt and pepper to taste, and serve immediately over the pork chops.

# Hidden Treasure

## Mark Holly

| | |
|---|---|
| 1 | English muffin, split |
| 2 | eggs |
| 1 to 2 | tablespoons butter |
| ⅓ | cup grated cheddar cheese |
| 4 | slices cooked bacon |

**Sauce**

| | |
|---|---|
| 4 | tablespoons tomato sauce |
| ½ | teaspoon salt |
| 1 | teaspoon fresh chopped garlic (or ½ teaspoon garlic powder) |
| 1 | teaspoon basil |
| ¼ | teaspoon oregano |
| ½ | teaspoon Tabasco |

Preheat oven to 350°. Toast the English muffin while cooking the bacon and preparing the sauce.

In a small (one-quart) saucepan, combine all of the sauce ingredients and cook over low heat for 5 to 8 minutes, or until mixture begins to simmer. Then turn the heat off and let stand until the Hidden Treasure is assembled and ready to be topped with the sauce.

Butter the bottom of a shallow baking dish. Butter both halves of the English muffin and place in the baking dish. Separate the eggs, place a yolk in the center of each muffin, and surround each yolk with half of the grated cheese. Whip the egg whites with a fork to a slightly fluffy consistency (or use a whisk or electric mixer for stiffer whites) and spread half on top of each muffin. Place bacon over the egg whites and top with a spoonful or two of the sauce. Bake for 10 to 12 minutes.

Place on plates with a fruit and parsley garnish, and complete the surprise with a bowl of fresh fruit and champagne cocktails—all, of course, served in bed.

*Mark Holly and Jill Hinckley*
*Hidden Treasure and champagne cocktails*

# Eggs Napoleon

## Gary Singer and Lorraine Craft

2 croissants
2 ounces ham, sliced
4 eggs, poached

### Hollandaise sauce

½ cup melted butter (one stick)
2 egg yolks
1 tablespoon lemon juice
dash cayenne pepper

paprika for garnish

Cut the croissants in half, lengthwise. Divide ham into four pieces and lay on the croissants. Warm ham and croissants on a cookie sheet or shallow baking pan in a 350° oven for 6 to 8 minutes while poaching eggs and making hollandaise sauce.

There is more than one way to poach an egg. One is to use a poaching pan with cups. You fill the bottom of the pan with water and bring to a boil. The steam will cook the eggs as they sit in the cups above the water. Melt a thin pat of butter in the cup, add the egg, cover, and cook for 3 to 5 minutes. The other way is to boil three or four inches of water in a two-quart saucepan. Break the egg into a bowl. Do not break the yolk. Turn the fire to low and stir the water to make it swirl in a circular motion. Slip an egg into the center of the swirl, poaching the eggs one at a time, for 3 to 5 minutes each. Remove the egg with a slotted spoon, and place on top of the ham on the croissant half.

Prepare the hollandaise sauce in the blender. Put the egg yolks, lemon juice, and cayenne pepper in the blender and blend. Continue to blend while slowly adding the melted butter. The heat from the butter will cook the egg, making the sauce thick, so be sure to have it hot. The sauce will be done when all the butter is added and blended in. Pour the hollandaise over the top of the eggs and sprinkle with paprika.

Serve immediately with fresh-brewed steaming coffee.

# Golden Rod

## Sam Irwin

⅓    **pound bacon (6 to 8 slices)**
4    **eggs, hard-boiled**

3    **tablespoons flour**
1½    **cups milk**
   **salt and pepper**

1    **small package of your favorite buttermilk biscuits,**
or 4    **fresh biscuits from your local bakery**

Fry the bacon until crisp and drain on paper towels. At the same time, boil the eggs. (Method for boiling eggs: Place the eggs in a one-quart saucepan and cover with cool water. Place on high heat uncovered. When the water just begins to simmer, turn heat to low, cover, and cook for 5 minutes, then remove from stove. Allow to stand until you begin the gravy. Pour out the hot water and run cool tap water over the eggs while they are still in the pan.)

Prepare the biscuits according to the package. If using bakery goods, warm them in a 275° oven. (Sam prefers his own scratch biscuits, but in the interest of having more time for loving by taking less time in the kitchen, the above alternatives work very well.)

Sam says the key to making gravy (and love) is to take it slow. Before starting the gravy, remove all but two to three tablespoons of the bacon drippings from the frying pan, but reserve the extra in a dish nearby. Add the flour to the drippings and stir over medium heat until the flour is well mixed into the bacon fat. (Hint: If the mixture is too thick and holds in clumps, add bacon drippings one teaspoonful at a time, stirring thoroughly in between. If the mixure is too thin, add flour in the same amount.) Continue to stir over medium heat for 3 or 4 minutes more to brown the mixture. Then, slowly add 1¼ cups of the milk while continuing to stir. The remaining ¼ cup should be used to adjust the consistency of the gravy to your preference. Salt and pepper to taste.

Crumble the bacon, peel and dice the eggs, and stir them both into the gravy. Split the biscuits open, lay them on plates, and spoon the Golden Rod gravy over the warm biscuits. Serve immediately with cantaloupe on the side.

# Migas (With Chips)

## Michael Young

| | |
|---|---|
| 2 | tablespoons butter |
| 1 | medium onion, diced |
| 2 | serrano peppers, seeded and finely chopped |
| 4 | eggs, beaten |
| ½ | cup grated cheese, cheddar or jack |
| 1 | medium tomato, diced |
| ½ to 1 | cup tortilla chips, crushed |

Sauté onion in butter. When onion begins to soften, add serrano peppers. Stir briefly and add eggs and cheese. Cook as you would scrambled eggs. When eggs achieve desired consistency, add tomato and chips, incorporate into the eggs, and serve immediately.

This is a time-saver dish. You just chop and add to the pan, chop and add. From first chop to serving time should take approximately 10 minutes.

The success of migas depends on the order in which you add the ingredients. The tomatoes in the finished dish should be firm and the chips slightly crisp, so they must go in last.

Serve with picante sauce on the side. Lovely with Bloody Marys!

*Mike likes to serve migas on the floor. It's a knee-to-knee, fun-filled experience while watching Saturday morning cartoons. For a late-night snack, he places the champagne bucket in the middle of the floor so he and a friend can huddle around it like a campfire.*

# Insane Eggs
## (Crazy for Your Yolks)
### Anonymous

| | |
|---|---|
| 6 to 8 | slices of bacon, cut in half-inch pieces |
| 1 | medium onion, diced |
| 1 | tablespoon butter |
| 1 | cup whole-kernel corn, frozen or canned and drained |
| 4 | eggs beaten |
| ½ | cup grated Jarlsburg cheese |
| ½ | jalapeño pepper, seeded and finely diced (not fresh) |
| ½ | cup black olives, sliced (optional) |

In a frying pan, brown the bacon slowly until almost crispy. Add the onion and sauté on medium heat until tender. Remove the bacon, onions, and one tablespoon of bacon grease to a clean frying pan so that the eggs will not be discolored with the browning from the bacon. Add butter and corn. If using canned corn, cook until the corn is warmed. If using frozen corn, sauté on medium heat until corn is done to taste. In a bowl, add the cheese, jalapeño pepper, and olives, if desired, to eggs and mix thoroughly, then add the mixture to the corn in the frying pan. Cook as you would scrambled eggs. (Note: Salt and pepper are not needed as the bacon adds enough salt and the jalapeño enough spice. )

Serve with fresh fruit and toasted English muffins or warmed flour tortillas. To up the octane rating on this breakfast, try it with Bloody Marys (page 124) or Mimosas (page 121).

Don't worry if there are leftovers. In fact, you may want to double the recipe so there will be leftovers. For a quick meal or snack, wrap leftover Insane Eggs in a flour tortilla and heat in the microwave.

*This is for those mornings when you skipped dinner, or when you had so much fun the night before that your head feels like it's about three feet above your neck. Guaranteed to satiate ravenous appetites.*

# AFTERNOON DELIGHT: LUNCHES AND PICNICS

Lunches usually have the same obstacle to overcome that breakfasts do—lack of time. And that's why quickies and fast food were invented. If you're planning a "sack" lunch, you'll want to spend as little time in the kitchen as possible. Some of the following recipes can be prepared in fifteen minutes or less, so you'll have time to do other things on your lunch hour. Give it some thought and plan ahead. Perhaps you can fix the dish the night before, or at least get some of the preparation out of the way.

If you are lucky enough to have a couple of hours for lunch, or you've called in sick, or you are planning your lunch for the weekend, you could be in for a real picnic. Some of these dishes are custom-made for romantic outings. You may have to go to just a bit more trouble to pack up a portable lunch, but if you keep it simple, it will all be worth it. Remember, even a blanket spread out in your own back yard can qualify as a romantic setting. Combine any lazy afternoon with one of these recipes, and there is no doubt that your special someone will want to get into your basket of goodies immediately.

# Fajitas

## Barbara and Bob Asmussen

1½    pounds trimmed skirt steak

### Marinade

1    cup salad oil
½    cup wine vinegar
¼    cup lemon juice
¼    cup Worcestershire sauce
1    tablespoon ground pepper
1    tablespoon garlic salt

### Guacamole

2    avocados, diced
½    lemon, juice only
½    cup sour cream
1    teaspoon garlic salt
¼    teaspoon cayenne pepper

### Grilled onions

2    medium onions, sliced
3    tablespoons oil
3    tablespoons soy sauce
½    teaspoon garlic salt
¼    teaspoon ground pepper

### Other toppings

1    cup grated cheddar or longhorn cheese
1    medium diced tomato
     sour cream

6 to 8    flour tortillas

The day before, tenderize the skirt steak by beating the meat vigorously on both sides with a meat hammer. Combine marinade ingredients, cover meat with marinade, and let stand in the refrigerator for at least 24 hours. Turn the meat three or four times during the marinating process. Bob says that the trick to the best fajitas

*Barbara and Bob Asmussen*
*Fajitas and cold beer*

is all in how you beat the meat. He recommends vigor and making sure you get all sides. Also, it's more fun when Barbara watches.

Grill meat over an open flame to desired doneness. Then, cutting across the grain of the meat, slice into half-inch-wide strips.

The guacamole should be prepared one hour in advance. Combine all ingredients in a glass bowl, mashing the avocado while mixing thoroughly, and adjust seasonings to taste. Allow to chill in refrigerator.

Grilled onions can be prepared while the meat is cooking. Break onions into individual rings. Combine with remaining ingredients in a large sauté pan over medium heat. Stir frequently until onions become limp—the only limp thing about fajitas.

Building the individual fajita is up to the person who gets to eat it, but the basic process is this: Take a flour tortilla, lay several hunks of meat across the middle, cover with cheese, guacamole, sour cream, tomatoes, and grilled onions, and fold the outer edges of the tortilla around the filling.

Serve with cold beer and your favorite chips.

*Texans tend to think of fajitas as the number-one alternative to barbecue when a crowd of hungry people needs to be fed, but they're also just right for an intimate little picnic. Whether you're serving two or twenty, fajitas are custom-made for a lazy afternoon, when time is the last thing on your mind.*

# Oriental Grilled Pork Chops

## *Raymond Tatum*

2    six- to eight-ounce pork chops

**Marinade**

½    cup soy sauce
3    tablespoons oriental sesame oil
1    tablespoon very finely chopped fresh ginger root
3 or 4    smashed cloves garlic
    juice of one lime
¼    cup rice vinegar

Combine marinade ingredients in a glass dish just large enough to hold the two pork chops, and marinate the pork chops for several hours (but no less than 2 hours). Turn periodically to fully marinate both sides. This marinade is also good with chicken.

Grill the pork chops over the hot fire of an open charcoal grill for 5 to 6 minutes on each side to desired doneness. While grilling the pork chops, transfer the marinade to a sauté pan and reduce over medium heat to about half the beginning amount to make the sauce.

Serve pork chops while piping hot, right off the grill, with the sauce on the side and your favorite rice or vegetable dish.

# Stuffed Quail (Smoked)

## Chef Emil

4      semi-boneless or whole quail
       salt and pepper
½      cup diced white onion
2      tablespoons duck fat or vegetable oil
       pinch each of dried rosemary, sage, and
           granulated garlic
½      cup diced apple
       dash apple brandy
1      cup cooked wild and long-grain rice blend
4      slices bacon

Quail should be available at the butcher shop or poultry vendor. Semi-boneless quail are ideal, because they are easier to eat, but whole quail are certainly just as delicious.

Rinse quail and lightly salt and pepper the inside cavity. In a medium (ten-inch) sauté pan, cook the onion in duck fat or oil over medium heat 4 to 5 minutes until translucent. Add herbs and apple, and cook over medium heat for 3 to 5 minutes more. Add the brandy and flame. After a minute or so, the flame will subside. Stir in wild rice (Uncle Ben's mix works fine) and let cool slightly. Stuff the quail, being careful not to tear the skin, cross the legs in front, and wrap completely with a strip of bacon.

Slow smoke the birds over hickory chips for approximately 1½ hours, or roast them in a 350° oven for 35 minutes. Smoking the birds will give them the added smoky flavor, as well as browning them more than the roasting method.

Stuffed quail can be served immediately, while still hot from the grill, or chilled for an afternoon outing. Serve with a chilled white Bordeaux wine.

*Emil and Judy Vogely*
*Stuffed Quail, Stuffed Summer Squash,*
*white wine, and grapes*

# Carne Asada Fresca

## Tony Villegas

| | |
|---|---|
| 1½ | pounds sirloin tip |
| ¼ | cup vegetable oil |
| 1 | large white onion, diced |
| 1 | large bell pepper, diced |
| 2 | large tomatoes, diced |

### Marinade

| | |
|---|---|
| ½ | cup soy sauce |
| ½ | cup lime juice (about four limes) |
| 1 | cup water |
| ¼ | cup oil |
| 1 | teaspoon garlic powder |
| ½ | onion, chopped |

The day before, cut the sirloin into quarter-inch-thick slices, combine all the marinade ingredients, and marinate the meat in the refrigerator for 24 hours.

To cook, preheat a large skillet over high heat. Remove the meat from the marinade. Add the oil to the hot skillet and swirl it around to cover the bottom. Add the meat immediately and brown for about 3 minutes. Add the bell pepper and onion. Sauté for another 2 to 3 minutes. Add the tomatoes and sauté until they are thoroughly heated.

Serve immediately with Spanish Rice, Avocado Salad (both on page 94), and a Margarita on the rocks (page 124).

*Tony and Denise Villegas*
*Carne Asada Fresca, Spanish Rice, and*
*Avocado Salad with Margaritas on the rocks*

# Mixed Caesar Salad
# With Seafood

### Horst Pfeifer, Gert Rausch

| | |
|---|---|
| 4 | large shrimp, peeled and deveined |
| 1 | lobster tail |
| 4 | scallops |
| 1 | cup white wine |
| ¼ | pound smoked salmon |
| ¼ | pound radicchio (Italian red chicory) |
| ½ | pound fresh spinach |
| 1 | small head romaine lettuce |

### Dressing

| | |
|---|---|
| 1 | teaspoon Dijon mustard |
| ¼ | cup red wine vinegar |
| 2 | tablespoons red wine (burgundy) |
| ¼ | cup olive oil |
| ¼ | cup vegetable oil |
| ¼ | teaspoon ground pepper |
| ⅛ | teaspoon salt |
| 1 | egg |
| ½ | teaspoon finely chopped anchovies |
| ½ | cup grated fresh Parmesan cheese |
| 1½ | teaspoons fresh finely chopped garlic |

Cut the shrimp and lobster into bite-size pieces and place in a small saucepan. Add the scallops and wine, and poach over low heat for 10 minutes or until just done. Drain and set aside to cool until ready to assemble.

In a large salad bowl, combine all of the dressing ingredients, thoroughly mix, and set aside. Wash and soak the radicchio in warm water for about 15 minutes to take out the bitterness. Clean the spinach and romaine lettuce in cold water. Drain off any excess water, tear the radicchio, spinach, and romaine into small pieces, and add to the salad bowl with the dressing in the bottom. Toss thoroughly.

Cut the smoked salmon into bite-size pieces. Toss greens once again and serve on plates or in salad bowls. Sprinkle half of the seafood on top of each salad. Serve with French bread and a red burgundy.

# Fettuccine Alfredo
## (Perking Up Limp Noodles)
### Michael Young


| | |
|---|---|
| 6 to 8 | cups boiling water |
| 1 | teaspoon salt |
| 1 | tablespoon olive oil |
| ¼ to ½ | pound fresh fettuccine pasta |

**Sauce**

| | |
|---|---|
| 2 | tablespoons butter |
| ⅓ | cup half-and-half |
| ¼ | cup freshly grated Parmesan cheese |
| | fresh ground pepper to taste |

Bring the water to a boil and add salt and olive oil. Allow water to recover to a full boil and add pasta. Boil pasta until just done. The true test is to taste. Pasta should be slightly firm, but without the chewy, floury taste. Drain in a colander.

Melt butter in sauté pan and add cream. Raise heat to medium or medium-high, and warm butter and cream until cream begins to rise in pan. Add cheese and slightly reduce heat, slowly stirring until cheese melts.

Add pasta to sauce and toss in the sauté pan until pasta is well mixed with sauce. Serve immediately with fresh pepper.

This dish must be prepared immediately before serving. It will not hold, so timing is important. The quality of this dish depends on the quality of the Parmesan cheese. For the consistency to be correct, the cheese should be melted and smooth, not grainy. Also, dried pasta may be used, but it will take a little longer to cook.

To add some snap to this lunch, try a chilled salad of romaine, grated carrot, avocado slices, and your favorite dressing, prepared while the water boils.

*Mike's preferred accompaniments are a crisp California chardonnay or a French white burgundy and tons of mail-order catalogs for a mad-cap, at-home shopping spree with his loved one. (That's how he recently acquired one thousand water balloons and a slingshot that will toss a water balloon up to one hundred yards.)*

# Crab-Stuffed Avocado

## Mark Holly

|       |                                    |
|-------|------------------------------------|
| 1     | ripe avocado                       |
| 1     | lemon                              |
| 4 to 6 | washed leaves of lettuce or spinach |

### Salad

|     |                                 |
|-----|---------------------------------|
| 4   | ounces lump crabmeat            |
| ½   | tomato, diced                   |
| 1   | tablespoon finely chopped celery |
| 1   | tablespoon chopped parsley      |

### Dressing

|     |                                                 |
|-----|-------------------------------------------------|
| ½   | cup mayonnaise                                  |
| ½   | cup crumbled blue cheese                        |
| 1   | teaspoon fresh chopped garlic or garlic powder  |
| 1   | teaspoon Worcestershire sauce                   |

Cut the avocado in half, remove the pit and peel. Cut the lemon in half lengthwise and use one half to make wedges for garnish. Squeeze the juice from the other half over the avocado.

Combine the salad ingredients in a small mixing bowl. In another small bowl, mix the dressing ingredients. Pour the dressing over the salad ingredients and toss together.

On two small plates, lay out the lettuce or spinach leaves. Put an avocado half on each plate and spoon the salad mixture into the cavity. Garnish with lemon wedges.

*This light, refreshing dish is just the thing for sleepy summer afternoons.*

*Mark Holly and Jill Hinckley*
*Crab-Stuffed Avocado, Asparagus in Prosciutto, and*
*Ramos Gin Fizz*

# Meat Loaf

## Barbara and Bob Asmussen

| | |
|---|---|
| 1½ | pounds lean ground beef |
| ½ | cup chopped onions |
| ½ | cup cracker crumbs |
| 3 | eggs |
| 8 | pimiento stuffed green olives, sliced |
| | dash salt and pepper |
| 2 | tablespoons Worcestershire sauce |

### Topping

| | |
|---|---|
| ½ | cup catsup |
| 1 | tablespoon Worcestershire sauce |
| ¼ | cup brown sugar |
| 1 | tablespoon soy sauce |

In a large mixing bowl, combine all of the meat loaf ingredients and mix thoroughly. Mold into the shape of a small loaf of bread and place in a shallow 10″ × 6″ (or approximate size) baking dish. Combine the topping ingredients in a small dish and pour over the top of the meat loaf. Bake in a preheated 350° oven for 1 hour. Remove to a serving plate and slice in desired thickness.

Serve with Candied Carrots (page 100) for a sweet addition to your meal.

# Redfish in Lemon Butter

## Raymond Tatum

| | |
|---|---|
| 2 | eight-ounce (average) fillets redfish |
| | salt and pepper |
| | flour, for dusting fillets |
| 2 | tablespoons oil |
| ½ | lemon |
| 1 | teaspoon chopped parsley |
| 4 | tablespoons butter |

Lightly salt and pepper the fillets, dust with flour, sauté in oil over medium-high heat 3 or 4 minutes on each side until done, and remove to plates. Clean the pan, add the juice of half a lemon, and bring to a boil over high heat. Count to five and turn off the burner, immediately add the butter and parsley, and swirl the pan until all the butter is melted and incorporated. Pour lemon butter sauce over the fillets and serve immediately.

This dish is truly a classic and also works well with other fish, such as trout, snapper, or flounder.

Serve with steamed and buttered vegetables and a crisp garden salad.

# Grilled Tuna Niçoise Salad

## Kate Hinds and Dave Meeks

| | |
|---|---|
| 1 | pound yellowtail tuna |
| 2 | medium new potatoes, boiled and sliced |
| ½ | pound green beans, trimmed and blanched |
| 2 | hard-boiled eggs, sliced into wedges |
| 1 | medium ripe tomato, sliced into wedges |
| ½ | green bell pepper cut into strips |
| ½ | red bell pepper cut into strips |
| ½ | Bermuda or red onion cut into very thin slices |
| 6 to 8 | anchovy fillets in olive oil |
| 8 to 10 | niçoise black olives or other small black olives |
| 1 | tablespoon chopped fresh basil |

### Marinade dressing

| | |
|---|---|
| 2 | teaspoons mustard |
| 2 | tablespoons wine vinegar |
| | juice from one lemon |
| 3 or 4 | cloves minced garlic |
| ¾ | cup olive oil |
| | salt and pepper |

Combine the marinade ingredients and marinate the tuna for half an hour before grilling. Prepare and light the charcoal for grilling. Boil the potatoes (about 20 minutes), beans (5 to 7 minutes), and eggs (about 5 minutes) until done. The potatoes, beans, and eggs can be cooked and chilled beforehand to carry on a picnic. This will leave you more time for conversation, champagne, and relaxing while waiting for the charcoal to get hot.

When the coals are ready, grill the tuna steaks for 4 to 6 minutes on each side (depending on the thickness) over a very hot fire. While the tuna is grilling, assemble the remaining salad ingredients. When the tuna is done, break the steaks into pieces and toss in the salad with the marinade dressing.

*Kate Hinds and Dave Meeks*
*Grilled Tuna Niçoise Salad and champagne*

# APPETEASERS

Appeteasers are for teasing an appetite and each other, for pricking the imagination to get things going, and maybe even running wild. They are an aphrodisiac for lovers of good food. They'll get the juices flowing—gastronomically speaking—and you just take care of the rest.

When serving an appeteaser, you need to select a provocative but comfortable setting, such as a hottub or bathtub, a private patio or balcony, a pile of pillows in front of the fireplace, or, if you really want to mix your pleasures, the bedroom.

To emphasize the sensual qualities of a fine dish, most of these recipes are made to be eaten with the most sensitive tools you have—the fingers. So don't be shy about dipping right in, but once you get started, eat slowly, savoring every bite.

A good appeteaser must be pleasing to the eye, and these recipes will certainly be that. They contain all the teasing temptation and visual stimulation any appetite could need.

# Shrimp Ceviche Salad

## Tony Villegas

| | |
|---|---|
| 1 | pound small to medium uncooked shrimp |
| 1 | cup fresh lime juice (6 to 8 limes) |
| | |
| 2 | large tomatoes |
| 1 | large white onion |
| 4 | fresh serrano peppers (more or less, depending on how hot you like it) |
| ½ | bunch fresh cilantro |
| ¼ | cup fresh lime juice |
| | salt |
| | |
| 1 | head iceberg lettuce |
| | |
| | grated cheddar cheese, avocado, and tomato for garnish |

Peel and devein uncooked shrimp and marinate overnight in the lime juice. Make sure that the shrimp is covered with the lime juice. If not, add more lime juice as needed. (For the chefs new to ceviche, the lime juice cooks the shrimp. You can tell when it is done by cutting across the thickest part of a shrimp. If the meat is white throughout, it is done. If there is still raw flesh in the center, allow the shrimp to marinate longer.)

Dice tomatoes, onion, peppers, and cilantro and mix in a large bowl. Drain the shrimp and add it to the mixture along with the quarter cup of lime juice. Stir and add salt to taste.

Serve over a bed of lettuce. Garnish with grated mild cheddar cheese, chunks of avocado, or slices of tomato. A chilled white wine is a nice complement.

*Tony and Denise Villegas*
*Shrimp Ceviche Salad, tostada chips,*
*and white wine*

# Quail Galantine With
# Orange Sauce and Pink Peppercorns

*Horst Pfeifer, Gert Rausch*

Two whole boneless quail

## Stuffing

| | |
|---|---|
| 6 | ounces ground veal |
| 1 | egg |
| ¼ | cup heavy whipping cream |
| 2 | ounces cooked fresh spinach (about ¼ cup) |
| 1 | ounce shelled pistachio nuts (about 3 tablespoons whole) |
| 1 | ounce cooked ham cut in quarter-inch cubes (about 3 tablespoons) |
| ¼ | teaspoon salt and pepper mixed |
| 1 | can chicken stock (14½ ounces) |

## Sauce

| | |
|---|---|
| | juice from two oranges |
| | grated peel of one orange |
| ⅛ | teaspoon pink peppercorns |
| or ¹⁄₁₆ | teaspoon green peppercorns (only if pink are not available) |
| ⅛ | teaspoon aspic (unflavored gelatin) |
| | dash cayenne pepper |

This should be prepared one day in advance. Blend veal with egg, cream, and spinach in a food processor or blender until it forms a thin dough. Remove and place in a chilled bowl. Add pistachio nuts, ham, and salt and pepper. Mix and refrigerate for at least 30 minutes. Stuff mixture inside quail. Place quail in a one-quart baking dish. Pour chicken stock over quail and cover with lid. Cook in a preheated 425° oven for 25 minutes. Remove from stock and cool in refrigerator for one day.

The sauce can be made a day in advance also. Put all the ingredients in a small saucepan and cook over medium heat for 10 minutes. Remove from heat and let cool to a gel.

To serve, slice the quail in two or three diagonal slices and place flat on a plate. Place two spoonfuls of orange sauce gel next to the quail and garnish with fresh fruit, such as sliced kiwi or strawberries.

# Stuffed Summer Squash

## Chef Emil

| | |
|---|---|
| 8 to 10 | crookneck summer squash (yellow, about four inches long) |
| 1 | six-ounce jar of marinated artichoke hearts |
| 2 | large cloves garlic |
| ⅓ | cup mayonnaise |
| | pinch diced parsley |
| 4 | ounces cream cheese |
| | dash seasoning salt |
| 1 | tablespoon Parmesan cheese, grated |
| 1 | tablespoon sour cream |
| | dash dry vermouth |
| ½ | teaspoon dill weed |

**finely chopped parsley for garnish**

Slice the tip off the fat end of the squash and parboil for 5 minutes or until soft. Chill immediately in ice water. With a small spoon or melon baller, scoop out the seeds. Drain open end down on paper towels in the refrigerator.

Prepare the two fillings as follows:

1. Blend the mayonnaise, one clove garlic (either finely diced or pushed through a garlic press), and a small pinch of parsley for color.

2. Let the cream cheese come to room temperature and blend with a clove of minced or pressed garlic, Parmesan cheese, seasoning salt, vermouth, dill, and sour cream.

Chill both fillings.

To assemble the squash, remove the artichoke hearts from the jar and let them drain for a minute. Trim if necessary and stuff the hearts into the squash, pushing them all the way into the cavity, flush with the edges. Fill a small tip pastry bag with the mayonnaise filling and cover the open end of half the squash with a floweret. Rinse the pastry bag and fill with cream cheese filling, repeating the process with the remaining squash. Dip the ends in parsley flakes and chill.

Arrange on a platter and serve with your favorite beverage, or serve as a side dish with Emil's Stuffed Quail (page 30) for a picnic lunch. *(Shown with the Stuffed Quail on page 31.)*

# Steak Tartare
## (In the Raw)
### Bobo Van Mechelen

| | |
|---:|:---|
| 1 | pound ground round |
| 2 | egg yolks |
| 2 | teaspoons Dijon mustard |
| 5 or 6 | capers (optional) |
| 2 | tablespoons Worcestershire sauce |
| 2 | medium shallots, finely chopped |
| 2 or 3 | dashes Tabasco sauce |
| 1 | tablespoon paprika |
| ¼ | cup vegetable oil (not olive oil—it is a bit too strong) |

cornichons (gherkins)
pickled onions
French bread

Steak tartare can be mixed by hand or in a food processor. If you use the food processor, be careful not to overgrind the meat.

Otherwise, making the tartare is simple. Just combine all the ingredients and mix thoroughly. Chill for about one hour in the refrigerator while the flavors blend.

Serve with cornichons, also called gherkins, and pickled onions. Spread the tartare on slices of French bread and enjoy it with a glass of red wine, either Beaujolais or Bordeaux. (Shown with the Lobster on page 69 molded in the shape of a heart.)

# Broiled Shrimp With Cashew Pesto

## Alan Lazarus

|        |                                                        |
|--------|--------------------------------------------------------|
| 8 to 10 | large shrimp                                          |
| 1      | tablespoon melted butter                               |

**Pesto**

|       |                                                         |
|-------|---------------------------------------------------------|
| 2     | cups fresh basil, packed                                |
| ½     | cup freshly grated Parmesan cheese                      |
| ⅓     | cup roasted cashews                                     |
| ¼     | cup olive oil                                           |
| 2     | tablespoons minced fresh garlic                         |
| ½     | teaspoon salt (delete if cashews are salted and salt to taste) |

lemon, Bermuda onion, and green
onion for garnish

To prepare the pesto, simply combine all the ingredients in a food processor or blender and grind to a paste.

Peel shrimp except for tail. Devein and butterfly the meat if desired. Baste with butter and place under broiler for 2 to 3 minutes. Turn and baste the other side with butter and cook for 2 to 3 minutes. The meat is done when it turns white to the center of the shrimp.

Spoon pesto on top of each shrimp and broil again for 20 seconds.

Arrange the shrimp on a plate or platter with garnishes and serve with a chilled dry white wine. (*Shrimp shown with Chilled Avocado and Crabmeat Soup on page 97.*)

# Shrimp Remoulade
*(For Your Fingers Only)*
*Dale Emmert*


8 to 12    large shrimp boiled and peeled
(do not remove the tails)

**Sauce**

| | |
|---|---|
| 1½ | cups mayonnaise |
| 2 | tablespoons creole or Dijon mustard |
| ½ | cup diced celery |
| ¼ | cup diced bell pepper |
| ½ | cup diced onion |
| 1 | teaspoon paprika |
| ½ | teaspoon cayenne pepper |
| 1 | tablespoon Worcestershire sauce |


To make sauce, mix all ingredients and let stand covered in refrigerator at least 4 hours before serving. You may also wish to prepare the sauce the day before.

If you do not already have a favorite method of boiling shrimp, Dale recommends using one quart of water, a teaspoon of salt (rock salt will add to the "sea" flavor), a stalk of celery cut into four or five large pieces, one quarter of a yellow or white onion left in a large piece, one whole bay leaf, juice from one lemon, two tablespoons cayenne pepper, and two tablespoons paprika. Bring all the ingredients to a hard boil, add the shrimp, cover, and remove the pan from the fire. Allow the shrimp to sit in the water for 3 to 4 minutes, then remove and drain them in a colander.

To present this dish with a flair, use a whole outer leaf of purple cabbage as a bowl. Fill it with shredded lettuce and arrange the shrimp in a pinwheel pattern on top, with plenty of remoulade sauce. Garnish with bell pepper, Italian pepper, and lemon wedges.

A red wine is recommended with this spicy sauce. Dale's preference is a cabernet sauvignon.

*Remember, you have four potentially glorious hours before this dish is served. Use your imagination. The shrimp are at their best when eaten with the fingers, preferably your partner's.*

*Dale and Debra Emmert*
*Shrimp Remoulade and red wine*

# Oysters With Horseradish

## Kate Hinds and Dave Meeks

| | |
|---|---|
| 1 | cup white wine |
| 1 | cup whipping cream |
| ¼ | cup cream-style horseradish |
| 4 or 5 | drops Worcestershire sauce |
| | cayenne pepper to taste |
| ½ | cup coarsely chopped celery |
| ½ | pint fresh shucked raw oysters |
| ½ | cup bread crumbs |
| ¼ | cup fresh chopped chives |

In a small, one-quart saucepan over medium heat, reduce white wine to one-quarter cup. Add the whipping cream and reduce until the mixture thickens. Stir in the horseradish, Worcestershire sauce, and cayenne pepper to taste. Remove from heat and allow mixture to cool.

Line a shallow baking dish with celery, place the oysters on the celery, spoon the sauce over the oysters, and sprinkle with bread crumbs. Bake in a preheated oven at 450° for 10 to 12 minutes until crumbs are brown and oysters bubble at the edges.

Garnish with chopped chives on top and serve immediately with well-chilled champagne.

# Shrimp-Stuffed Mushrooms

## Mark Holly

|       |                                                                                                  |
|-------|--------------------------------------------------------------------------------------------------|
| 12    | medium fresh mushrooms                                                                            |
| 2     | tablespoons chopped celery                                                                        |
| 2     | tablespoons chopped bell pepper                                                                   |
| 2     | tablespoons chopped onion                                                                         |
| 1 or 2 | tablespoons oil                                                                                  |
| ½     | cup raw shrimp cut in small pieces (about four ounces without shell or six ounces with shell)     |
| ½     | teaspoon pepper                                                                                   |
| 1     | tablespoon finely chopped garlic                                                                  |
| ⅓     | cup Parmesan cheese                                                                               |
| ¾     | cup butter                                                                                        |
| 1     | tablespoon lemon juice                                                                            |

Preheat the oven to 400°. Clean mushrooms, remove and save the stems, and place mushroom caps in a baking dish. Chop the stems and combine them with the celery, bell pepper, onion, and oil in a sauté pan. Cook over medium heat until the vegetables are soft, about 5 to 6 minutes. Add the shrimp, pepper, and garlic and cook for 2 to 3 minutes until shrimp is done, stirring frequently.

Spoon the shrimp mixture into the mushroom caps, and sprinkle with Parmesan cheese. Melt the butter, add the lemon juice to the butter, and pour over the mushrooms. Bake for 8 to 10 minutes at 400° or until cheese is browned slightly.

# Stuffed Artichokes
## (Get to the Heart of the Matter)
### Barbara and Bob Asmussen

| 2 | fresh artichokes |
|---|---|
| 1 | stick melted butter |

**Stuffing**

| 1 | cup dried bread crumbs |
|---|---|
| 1 | tablespoon Italian seasoning |
| ½ | teaspoon garlic salt |
| | *or* |
| 1 | cup seasoned dried bread crumbs |

With scissors, snip the sharp tips from each artichoke leaf. Cut stem even with base of the artichoke. Boil in lightly salted water approximately 10 minutes, until tender.

In a small bowl, combine the stuffing ingredients and mix thoroughly. (If you use seasoned bread crumbs, you do not need to use the Italian seasoning or garlic salt.) Spoon the dry stuffing mix behind every leaf of the artichoke. Place the artichokes in a foil-lined baking dish, pour melted butter over them to saturate the stuffing mix behind each leaf, and bake for 25 minutes in a preheated 375° oven.

Serve on large plates so there is room for the discard or on small plates with one large plate to share for the discard. Garnish with lemons or other colorful edibles, such as radish flowers or carrot curls.

Any wine is fine with this dish, and when it's real cold outside, Bob and Barbara like it with Irish coffee.

*Bob and Barbara Asmussen*
*Stuffed Artichokes with Irish coffee*

# Ceviche

## (Fishing for Compliments)
### Michael Young

| | |
|---|---|
| ½ | pound fresh redfish, cut into half-inch cubes |
| 3 or 4 | fresh limes |
| 1 | medium onion, diced |
| 3 | sprigs cilantro, chopped |
| 1 | medium tomato, diced |
| 1 | medium avocado, diced |
| | salt and pepper to taste |

In a glass bowl or jar, combine the fish with lime juice. Be sure to add enough lime juice to completely cover the fish. Marinate fish 5 to 7 hours, thoroughly mixing two or three times during the process. The lime juice is what cooks the fish. When it's done the fish should be milky white all the way through.

Add onion and cilantro for the last hour or so of the marinating process. Add tomato and avocado just before serving.

Serve with crackers or tostada chips and a cold beer.

*Plan on a big kiss or two—your love will pucker up for you and this ceviche.*

# Stuffed Roasted Pimientos

## Mark Yznaga

| | |
|---|---|
| 2 | fresh pimientos (If fresh pimientos are not in season, you can use red, yellow, or even green bell peppers for a flavorful variation.) |
| 2 | anchovy fillets |
| ¼ | cup olive oil |
| ¼ | cup grated Parmesan or Romano cheese |
| 4 | cloves crushed garlic |
| | black pepper to taste |
| 4 | tablespoons fresh chopped parsley |

The first step is to roast the pimientos, which can be done in two ways. The best way is to roast them over an open grill using tongs to turn them. The other way is to cut them in half and place the cut side down on a pan under the broiler. Either way, you want to char the skin of the pimiento—that's right, turn it black. This should take only 5 to 10 minutes. Peel the charred skin off and cut the pimiento into slices one or two inches wide to form little long, thin boats.

Combine the remaining ingredients in a small bowl, mix thoroughly, and spoon into the sliced pimientos.

Some may consider this a very rich appetizer. Along with the Souvlaki and Humus bi Tahini from this chapter and the Stuffed Zucchini on page 88, it makes a complete meal. It's excellent with red wine.

# Chilled Smoked Shrimp
## and Orange Ginger Barbecue Sauce

*Jeff and Debby Blank*

| | |
|---|---|
| 1 | pound fresh jumbo shrimp, peeled and deveined |
| 1½ | cups sour cream |
| ¼ | cup fresh diced mixed herbs (equal parts of basil, oregano, sage, rosemary, thyme) |
| ⅓ | teaspoon salt |
| 2 | tablespoons white wine |

### Orange ginger barbecue sauce

| | |
|---|---|
| 3 | strips bacon, diced |
| ½ | white onion, diced |
| ½ | cup ready-made barbecue sauce |
| ½ | cup fresh orange juice |
| 2 | tablespoons orange zest |
| 3 | tablespoons brown sugar |
| 1½ | teaspoons fresh finely minced ginger (1 teaspoon dried) |
| | salt and pepper to taste |

Jeff advises preparing this dish a day or two in advance. The smoking process will prolong the freshness of the shrimp, and the flavors in the sauce will have a chance to mingle.

To begin, start a charcoal fire and soak some mesquite or hickory chips in water. Mix the sour cream, herbs, salt, and white wine. Add the shrimp and mix. There should be only a thin coating on the shrimp. If the mixture is too thick, thin it with a little white wine. When the fire is ready, add the wood chips to the fire, put the shrimp on skewers with half an inch between them, and grill until done. Be sure to turn often, as seafood cooks quickly. Chill the shrimp in the refrigerator.

### Sauce

In an eight- or ten-inch sauté pan, cook the bacon over medium heat until it begins to crisp. Add the onion and continue to cook until the onion becomes translucent. Remove the onion and bacon from the pan and in a small, one-quart bowl combine them with the remaining sauce ingredients and mix. Chill the sauce in the refrigerator.

Serve the chilled shrimp with sauce on the side as a dip. Accompany them with fresh fruits and Sangria (recipe on page 121). To keep the cut fruits from browning, dip them in a fifty/fifty mixture of water and lemon juice.

# Humus bi Tahini

## Mark Yznaga

| | |
|---|---|
| ¾ | cup tahini (sesame paste) |
| ½ | cup lemon juice (about two lemons) |
| 1 | cup drained chick-peas (garbanzos) |
| ½ | cup olive oil |
| ½ | cup orange juice |
| 4 | medium cloves crushed garlic |
| ½ | teaspoon red pepper or cayenne |
| | salt to taste |
| ¾ | cup fresh chopped parsley |

Blend the tahini with the lemon juice in a blender, gradually adding the chick-peas. The mixture should be very thick. Add the orange juice and olive oil until the mixture becomes smooth and creamy. Add the garlic, red pepper, and salt, correcting the seasonings as desired. Add about half of the parsley, reserving the remainder for garnish, and blend. Be careful not to blend too long. You want to distribute the parsley in the mixture, but it should remain recognizable.

Pour the mixture into a small serving dish and garnish with red pepper or paprika and the remaining parsley.

This is an excellent dip for small triangles of pita bread or with sliced fresh vegetables. Although it is not traditionally eaten with meat, it's good with such dishes as the Souvlaki on the next page.

# Souvlaki, Cypriot Style

## Mark Yznaga

1     pound pork shoulder or butt
½     cup olive oil
½     cup red wine
2     cloves crushed garlic
½     cup chopped parsley (reserve small amount
       for garnish)
       pinch salt and pepper
2     pita bread pockets
       chopped lettuce, tomato, cucumber, parsley
       plain yogurt

Cut the pork into two-inch cubes, leaving some of the fat on. Put the meat on skewers, placing the fat side of one cube to the lean side of the next. This will keep the meat moist as it cooks. Mix the olive oil, red wine, garlic, parsley (except amount reserved for garnish), and salt and pepper in a small bowl. Brush the mixture on the pork as you grill it to desired doneness over coals.

Cut the pita pockets in half (to form two pockets from each), brush the inside of the pocket with olive oil, and fold the pocket over the meat during the last minutes of cooking. This will flavor the pita bread with smoke. Remove from grill, and hold the pita around the meat while removing the skewer.

Serve with chopped lettuce, cucumbers, tomato, plain yogurt, and parsley. Try this with a little Humus bi Tahini (previous page). It adds a nice zing to the flavors.

# CANDLELIGHT SPECIALS: ENTRÉES

Evening dining affairs should offer a couple a thoroughly relaxing atmosphere in which to enjoy a meal and each other. You have both been in the ring fighting the cold cruel world all day long, and it is time to take off the gloves and enjoy the tranquility of your own little corner. So make it easy for yourself.

The linen tablecloth and napkins, the crystal, the fine china and silver, are nice but not necessary. The most important ingredients are candles and low lights, soft music, good wine, any one of these tantalizing dishes, and you.

With each savory mouthful your lover takes, you'll be scoring maximum points. As you will soon discover, these entrées are easy, even those that may at first appear more involved. So don't be afraid to try them.

The sauces are savory. The flavors are fulfilling. They will make you both purr with contentment.

# Truche de Amor
## (Love Trout)
### Chef Emil

| | |
|---|---|
| 1 | Gulf speckled trout, preferably 14 to 18 ounces |
| or 2 | rainbow trout, 8 to 10 ounces each |

### Stuffing

| | |
|---|---|
| 1½ | cup Magic Mix (see below) |
| ¼ | cup clarified butter |
| pinch | each of dried oregano, thyme, cayenne |
| ¼ | teaspoon minced garlic |
| dash | dry sherry |
| dash | lemon juice |
| ½ | cup fresh blue crabmeat |
| 1 | tablespoon fresh Parmesan cheese, grated |
| 3 | tablespoons bread crumbs, dried |

### Lemon Butter

| | |
|---|---|
| ½ | stick butter |
| | juice of one lemon |
| pinch | chopped parsley |
| ¼ | cup dry white wine |

This dish is spectacular, the sort of thing that sets off fireworks at an anniversary or Valentine's dinner. It takes some extra time and planning, so you'll want to save it for a very special occasion. This is best prepared as the single large speckled trout, but those trout are only intermittently available. The rainbow trout will certainly be as impressive.

To fillet the trout, remove the gills, stomach, throat, and belly meat. With a sharp knife, start at a point just behind the head and slice down the back on both sides of the top fin to just above the tail, being careful to keep the skin intact. Continue cutting through the fish until all the meat has been removed from the bone, but leave the head and tail attached to the two resulting fillets. With a sharp pair of scissors cut the backbone just behind the head and in front of the tail, and remove and discard the skeleton. This should leave you with a whole boneless fish. Wash and scale the fish if necessary. (You may want your fish market to do this step for you.)

To make the Magic Mix, finely dice and combine three parts celery (¾ cup), two parts onion (½ cup), and one part bell pepper (¼ cup).

To make the stuffing, sauté the Magic Mix in butter with the oregano, thyme, cayenne, and garlic until the vegetables are soft. Splash with sherry and

lemon juice and cook for 2 minutes more. Remove from heat and add the crabmeat. Add the Parmesan cheese and stir in the bread crumbs until the liquid is absorbed and the stuffing sticks together.

To prepare the trout, place the fish on its stomach on a buttered baking dish and let the fillets fall open skinside down. Then fold the tail underneath itself, toward the head and up through the middle—through the circle formed by the two sides of the fish. This will raise the sides of the fish so they stand up perpendicular to the dish and form a heart-shaped cavity. Fill the cavity with the stuffing and remold the fish into a heart shape. You may need to use some toothpicks to pull the tail section of the fillets together since the meat may be thin there. Bake at 400° for about 15 minutes or until a fork passes through the flesh without resistance. Allow to cool for 3 to 4 minutes while preparing the lemon butter and then transfer to a serving platter.

For the garnish, bring the lemon juice, wine, and parsley to a boil over high heat in a sauté pan, then remove from heat and add the butter in small pats. Swirl the butter into the liquid until it melts and the sauce thickens. Garnish the serving platter by pouring the lemon butter around the fish, cover the eyes with slices of black olives, and arrange sprigs of parsley in the top of the heart. Serve with Emil's Chilled Asparagus salad (page 101) and a chilled rosé or white wine.

# Lobster With Special Red Sauce and Homemade Mayonnaise

## Bobo Van Mechelen

| | |
|---|---|
| 2 | one-pound live lobsters |
| ¾ | gallon of water (3 quarts) |

### Seasonings

| | |
|---|---|
| ¾ | liter dry white wine (about 3 cups) |
| ½ | pound white onions |
| 1 | bunch celery |
| 1 | teaspoon salt |
| 4 | turns of the pepper mill |
| 2 | teaspoons thyme |
| 2 | bay leaves |

Plan to start the lobsters at least 2 hours before you serve them. The cooling process described below is essential to this boiling method, and ample time should be allowed.

Put the water in a large pot and bring to a boil. While waiting for the water to boil, peel and thick slice the onions. Wash the celery and cut the stalks and leafy ends into large (two-inch) pieces. When the water is boiling, add all of the seasonings to the water and continue to boil for 5 minutes.

Rinse the lobsters in running water. Put them in the boiling water, cover, and cook no longer than 10 minutes. Immediately remove the pot from the burner, uncover, and allow lobsters to cool to room temperature in the seasoned water. This should take about 2 hours.

Cut lobsters in half lengthwise and serve with the Homemade Mayonnaise and Special Red Sauce as dips, French bread and butter, and a chilled bottle of brut champagne.

## Homemade Mayonnaise

1 egg yolk
2 teaspoons Dijon mustard
1 cup vegetable oil
1 teaspoon lemon juice
  salt and pepper

Allow all of your ingredients to come to room temperature before beginning. In a mixing bowl, combine the egg yolk and mustard, beating with a hand whisk or an electric mixer. Slowly add the oil, a trickle at a time, while continuing to beat vigorously. (If you are beating by hand, you may have to add the oil intermittently.) As you add the oil, the mixture will thicken and take on body. Continue to beat vigorously, or on high speed, until all the oil is incorporated, then stir in the lemon juice and salt and pepper to taste.

## Special Red Sauce

½ of the Homemade Mayonnaise from above
⅓ cup catsup
2 tablespoons Scotch whisky
½ teaspoon paprika (more if desired)

Divide the above mayonnaise recipe in half, combine with the remaining Special Red Sauce ingredients, and mix thoroughly. And when the temptation arises to take a nip of the Scotch, don't forget that you will be having champagne with your love and the lobster.

*Bobo and Janice Van Mechelen*
*Lobsters, Steak Tartare, French bread,*
*and red wine*

# Veal Rolled With
# Fontina Cheese and Prosciutto

## Kate Hinds and Dave Meeks

| | |
|---|---|
| 4 | slices top round veal, three or four ounces each |
| ½ | finely chopped onion |
| 4 | tablespoons olive oil (split 2 and 2) |
| 2 | tablespoons finely chopped fresh sage leaves (split 1½ and ½) |
| 4 | slices fontina cheese |
| 4 | slices prosciutto ham, paper thin |
| 2 to 3 | heaping tablespoons flour |
| | dry marsala wine (amount depends on size of sauté pan) |
| 3 | tablespoons heavy (whipping) cream |
| | black pepper to taste |

**Pasta**

| | |
|---|---|
| 1 | small package taglionini, tagliatelle, or your favorite pasta |
| 1½ to 2 | quarts water |
| 1 | tablespoon salt |

With a meat hammer, pound the veal to less than a quarter inch thick. In a small (eight-inch) sauté pan, sauté the onions in 2 tablespoons of the olive oil over medium heat until soft. Remove from heat and add 1½ tablespoons of the sage. Layer the onion, cheese, and prosciutto on the veal and roll together, securing with a toothpick.

Reheat the sauté pan; add the remaining 2 tablespoons olive oil. Lightly dust the veal rolls with flour, place them in the pan, and brown on all sides over medium-high heat. Pour in the marsala, enough to come halfway up on the veal rolls. Lower the heat, cover, and cook for 10 minutes, turning the rolls occasionally. Then, remove the veal rolls to a warm dish. Reduce the marsala over medium heat to about half a cup or more of liquid, until it thickens slightly. Add cream, swirl it around in the pan, and allow it to reduce for another minute or two. Add the remaining ½ tablespoon of sage and black pepper to taste.

Cook the pasta according to the package instructions, drain, toss with 1 to 2 tablespoons of the veal sauce, and transfer pasta to a serving platter. Place the veal rolls on top of the pasta and pour the sauce over the rolls. Serve with Kate and Dave's favorite, champagne.

# Chicken Parmesan

## Gary Singer and Lorraine Craft

2    whole boneless chicken breasts
    without skin, in four halves

### Stuffing

2    cups dried bread crumbs
¾    cup melted butter
¼    cup water
¼    cup chopped celery
2    tablespoons chopped onion
1    teaspoon rosemary
½    teaspoon white pepper
½    teaspoon minced garlic

### Sauce

2    cups ultrapasteurized whipping cream
¼    teaspoon rosemary
1    chicken bouillon cube
¼    teaspoon white pepper
2    tablespoons flour
2    tablespoons butter

### Topping

½    cup fresh grated Parmesan cheese
½    cup cracker crumbs
¼    cup pecan pieces

With a meat hammer, beat each chicken breast half to a quarter inch or less in thickness. Combine the stuffing ingredients, mix thoroughly, put one fourth of the stuffing in the center of each chicken piece, and pull chicken over the stuffing to form a ball. Arrange the balls in an 8″ × 8″ baking dish, bake in a preheated 350° oven for 10 minutes, and remove from oven.

The sauce can be prepared in the first 10 minutes while the chicken is cooking. In a one-quart saucepan, bring the cream to a boil and add the rosemary, chicken bouillon, and pepper. In a ten-inch sauté pan, combine the butter and flour to make a roux and cook over medium heat for 3 or 4 minutes. Slowly pour the hot cream mixture into the roux while constantly stirring. Let simmer for 5 minutes.

Pour the sauce over the chicken balls, sprinkle liberally with Parmesan cheese, cracker crumbs, and pecan pieces. Return to the oven until bubbling and slightly brown on top (about 10 to 12 minutes).

# Lobster-Stuffed Lamb Chop in Pastry With Red Buttersauce

*Horst Pfeifer, Gert Rausch*

| | |
|---|---|
| 1 to 1½ | pound lamb rack (six to eight rib bones) |
| 1 | small (six- to eight-ounce) cooked lobster tail |
| 1 | tablespoon butter |
| 1 | cup cooked fresh spinach |
| 1 | shell puff pastry (frozen piecrust) |
| 1 | egg yolk (beaten lightly with a fork) |

### Sauce

| | |
|---|---|
| 2 | cups red burgundy |
| 1 | teaspoon finely chopped shallots |
| ¼ | teaspoon fresh rosemary |
| | salt and pepper |
| ½ | cup butter |

As though you were going to skewer the lamb rack lengthwise through the tenderloin, make a vertical and horizontal (crosscut) incision through the middle of the rack loin with a knife and stuff the cooked lobster tail into the loin. Grill the rack for 10 to 15 minutes to desired doneness, basting occasionally with butter. Cook the loin medium rare to medium for best flavor and texture. Remove from grill and allow to cool.

Place half of the spinach on top of the pastry in a thin layer the size of the loin. Place the rack on top of the spinach. Spread the remaining spinach on top of the rack, and close the pastry around the rack, leaving the tips of the bones exposed and using the egg yolk to seal the pastry. When completed, brush the pastry with the egg yolk and bake in a preheated oven at 450° for 20 minutes. Slice the rack between each rib and serve with sauce spooned on the side.

## Sauce

Cook the burgundy and shallots over medium-high heat until the liquid has been reduced to approximately a quarter cup. Add the fresh rosemary and salt and pepper to taste. Whisk in the butter until the sauce thickens. Remove immediately from heat.

Spinach Soufflé, Gratin Dauphinoise (both on page 90), and a dry red wine are excellent complements to this impressive dish.

*Gert Rausch and a friend*
*Lobster-Stuffed Lamb Chop, Spinach Soufflé,*
*Gratin Dauphinoise, and red wine*

# Chicken Breasts in
# Mushroom Red Wine Sauce

### Raymond Tatum

|          |                                           |
|----------|-------------------------------------------|
| 2        | whole boneless chicken breasts with skin  |
|          | salt and pepper                           |
|          | flour, for dusting the chicken breasts    |
| 2        | tablespoons vegetable oil                 |
| 3        | tablespoons butter                        |
| ½        | onion, sliced in semicircles              |
| 8 to 10  | mushrooms, sliced                         |
| ¾        | cup red wine                              |
| 2        | tablespoons red wine vinegar              |
| 4        | tablespoons butter                        |

Lightly salt and pepper the chicken breasts, dust with flour, and sauté over medium-high heat in vegetable oil for 3 or 4 minutes on each side until done. To determine doneness, touch the meat with your finger. You are looking for firm but not hard chicken. If it's too soft, the chicken needs to cook longer. When done, remove the chicken from skillet and clean the pan for the sauce.

Over medium-high heat, melt the three tablespoons of butter and add the onion and mushrooms to the pan. Add the red wine and vinegar and reduce for 5 to 8 minutes to one fourth of the original amount of liquid. Turn the fire off, add the four tablespoons of butter, and swirl in the pan until the butter is incorporated. The butter mixes in better if it is sliced into patties first.

Pour sauce over chicken breasts and serve immediately.

# Pork With Jezebel Sauce

## Barbara and Bob Asmussen

|   |   |
|---|---|
| 2 | eight-ounce boneless butterfly pork chops |
| 3 | heaping tablespoons flour |
|   | oil |
|   | salt and pepper |

**Sauce**

|   |   |
|---|---|
| 2 | cups fresh, frozen, or canned sliced apples |
| 1 | cup sugar |
| ¼ | cup brown sugar |
| ½ | cup butter |
| ½ | cup canned crushed pineapple |
| 2 | tablespoons horseradish |

Sauce should be started about 45 minutes ahead of the pork chops. Combine all the sauce ingredients in a one-and-a-half-quart saucepan, cover, and simmer over low heat for about 1 hour, until apples break down.

Dust pork chops with flour. Thoroughly heat a quarter inch of oil in a saucepan on high heat. Add pork chops and fry for 8 to 10 minutes on each side until done. Pierce with knife to inspect centers for doneness. Remove and drain on paper towels. Lightly salt and pepper both sides. Remove to serving dish, pour Jezebel sauce over chops, and serve while warm. Garnish with lemon wedges.

These pork chops are wonderful with Candied Carrots (page 100) and fresh steamed and buttered broccoli. Excellent with a chilled rosé wine.

For a variation try a pork roast with Jezebel sauce.

*While the sauce is simmering, the cooks need to entertain each other. Barbara likes to open the bottle of wine early and share a glass or two with Bob. As little time as they have together, she says it's a rare chance for them to—talk?*

# Mesquite-Grilled Venison Tenderloin
## (On the Wilder Side)
### Jeff and Debby Blank

| | |
|---|---|
| 1 | one-pound (average) venison tenderloin (backstrap) |
| 1 | cup crushed walnuts |
| 1 | teaspoon salt |
| ½ | teaspoon white pepper |

Start the charcoal and soak your mesquite chips. Clean the tenderloin by removing all silver skin, fat, or gristle.

Walnuts can be crushed in a food processor or blender. Mix the salt and pepper with the walnuts, sprinkle the walnuts on a piece of waxed paper, and roll the tenderloin in the mixture. The crushed walnuts should stick to the outside of the tenderloin. Wrap the meat in the waxed paper and refrigerate until the coals are ready.

When the coals are ready, add the mesquite chips. Grill the venison until medium rare, and remove it from the grill.

Allowing the tenderloin to cool for 3 to 4 minutes will make it easier to slice. Slice the tenderloin crosswise against the grain into medallions and fan them out across the plate. Serve with Stir-fry Vegetable Medley (page 91), red wine, low lights, and a cozy fire.

*Jeff and Debby Blank*
*Mesquite-Grilled Venison,*
*Stir-Fry Vegetable Medley, and red wine*

# Bourbon Street Chicken
## (Double-Breasted Delight)
### Dale Emmert


| 2 | double chicken breasts |
|---|---|

**Sauce**

| 2 | tablespoons butter |
|---|---|
| 3 | tablespoons flour, heaping |
| 1½ | cups heavy cream |
| 2 | beef bouillon cubes |
| ¼ | cup green Cajun peppercorns, or soft green peppercorns in brine |
| 2 | green onions, white part only, whole |
| | white pepper |
| | salt to taste |
| dash | paprika |
| sprig | parsley |

Grill chicken breasts over an outdoor grill or stove-top grill for 6 to 8 minutes on each side until done. It may be simpler to pan fry in unsalted butter over medium-high heat, but the flavor will differ slightly. Test for doneness by piercing thickest part of breast with knife; the meat inside should just be turning white. Be careful not to overcook.

Over low heat, make a medium-thick roux by melting butter and adding flour. Stir continuously for about 5 minutes, being careful not to brown. Add the bouillon cubes and slowly add cream, continuing to stir to a smooth, creamy consistency. Stir in green onions and green peppercorns. Add salt and white pepper to taste. Remove green onions and ladle sauce over grilled, piping hot chicken breasts. Garnish with a dash of paprika and a sprig of parsley.

Serve with Dale's Quick Salad (page 100) and a vegetable, such as steamed and buttered fresh long asparagus or a California blend of steamed cauliflower, broccoli, and carrots, buttered and salted to taste. Delicious with a chilled dry white wine.

# Pork Ardennaise

## Jean-Louis and Marie-Anne Dehoux

2    one-inch-thick pork chops with the bone
2    thick slices of smoked or cooked ham
2    thick slices of Swiss cheese
1    egg white
1    cup bread crumbs
     salt and pepper to taste
2    tablespoons clarified butter

Cut the pork chops in half horizontally, like a layer cake or a sandwich. Leave the meat attached at the bone; it will hold together better when cooking. Place a slice of ham and a slice of cheese in each pork chop.

Lightly beat the egg white in a small shallow bowl. Dip the pork chops in the egg white and then in the bread crumbs. Salt and pepper the pork chops to taste. Put the butter in a sauté pan or skillet and melt over medium-high heat, then add pork chops. After 2 or 3 minutes, turn the chops, reduce the heat to medium-low, and cover the pan. After 10 to 12 minutes, turn the chops a second time and continue to cook for another 10 to 12 minutes until done. If most of the juices have disappeared by the second turn, add a tablespoon or two of water to keep the chops from burning.

The Dehouxs recommend serving this with the Bean Sprouts in Soy Sauce on page 92 and Mashed Potatoes with Swiss Cheese on page 93. (Toss the leftover egg yolk in the mashed potatoes for added body and flavor.) Set the meal off with a hearty burgundy wine.

# Baked Whole Red Snapper With Saffron

*Kate Hinds and Dave Meeks*

|        |                                          |
|--------|------------------------------------------|
| 1      | two-pound (average) fresh whole red snapper |
| 1      | medium onion, sliced                     |
| 2      | tablespoons olive oil                    |
| ½      | green bell pepper, cut in strips         |
| ½      | red bell pepper, cut in strips           |
| 4      | cloves finely chopped garlic             |
| 2      | ripe tomatoes cut in wedges              |
| pinch  | saffron threads                          |
| 2      | cups white wine                          |
| 2      | tablespoons fresh chopped basil          |
| 1      | tablespoon fresh chopped thyme           |
| 2      | tablespoons Pernod                       |
|        | zest of one fourth of an orange          |
|        | salt and pepper to taste                 |

Preheat oven to 375°. Sauté onion in olive oil until wilted, add the peppers, garlic, tomatoes, saffron, and white wine, and mix thoroughly. Place whole snapper in a 9″ × 13″ × 2″ glass baking dish, pour the wine mixture over the fish, and bake for 20 to 25 minutes until done. Remove fish to a warm serving platter and pour the juices back into the sauté pan. Reduce over high heat by about half to concentrate the flavors. Add the herbs, orange zest, and Pernod, swirl in, and pour over the fish.

Serve immediately with a salad, rice, French bread, and champagne.

If you take a few seconds to arrange the orange zest on the body of the fish and the colorful vegetables on the platter, you'll have a visually striking creation as well as a delicious meal.

*Kate Hinds and Dave Meeks*
*Baked Whole Red Snapper With Saffron,*
*Green Bean Vinaigrette Salad, and champagne*

# Lamb Chops With
# Green Peppercorn Butter

## Raymond Tatum

| | |
|---|---|
| 4 | four- to five-ounce lamb chops |
| 2 | chopped shallots |
| 2 or 3 | chopped garlic cloves |
| 16 | green peppercorns |
| 1 | cup red wine |
| ¼ | cup red wine vinegar |
| dash | salt and pepper |
| ¾ | stick butter, softened to room temperature |
| 1 | tablespoon Dijon mustard |

Combine the shallots, garlic, half of the green peppercorns, wine, vinegar, and salt and pepper in a sauté pan. Simmer over medium heat until almost all liquid has evaporated, leaving only 2 or 3 tablespoons of liquid, and remove from the burner to cool. Then, put the butter in a small mixing bowl and add the contents of the pan, along with the remaining green peppercorns and the mustard. With a whisk or electric mixer, whip the ingredients together to finish the peppercorn butter.

Lightly salt and pepper the lamb chops and cook over a charcoal grill, or pan fry in oil or clarified butter, to medium rare or desired doneness, and remove from grill. Spread with the peppercorn butter and serve immediately with a baked potato or a vegetable.

Peppercorn butter is excellent on steaks and pork chops, also.

# Steak au Poivre à la Crème

*(Pepper Steak)*
**Bobo Van Mechelen**

| | |
|---|---|
| 2 | eight-ounce tenderloins |
| | salt and pepper |
| 1 | tablespoon butter |
| 1½ | ounces cognac |
| 1 | tablespoon Dijon mustard |
| ¼ | teaspoon arrowroot |
| 1 | cup whipping cream |
| 20 | twists of the pepper mill (about 1 tablespoon) |

In a skillet large enough to lay the tenderloins side by side, heat the butter on high, add the tenderloins when pan is hot, cook to medium rare or desired doneness, and salt and pepper to taste. Remove to a heated plate or place in the oven on low heat (about 250°), while making the pepper cream gravy.

Add the mustard, arrowroot, and cognac to the pan and stir over medium heat with a whisk, bringing the mixture to a simmer. Expect the mixture to thicken and slightly darken. Turn the heat to low and keep stirring with the whisk as you slowly add the cream. Continue to whisk or the gravy will separate. Allow it to simmer slowly for another 10 to 12 minutes to allow the gravy to reduce and thicken. When the gravy has reached the desired consistency, add the pepper, whisk it through the gravy, and serve over the steaks immediately.

Pepper steak is best when served with a red burgundy wine and shoestring french fries. Beforehand, you may wish to have a small green salad with a vinaigrette dressing of oil, vinegar, Dijon mustard, and salt and pepper, mixed to your taste.

Shoestring french fries are difficult to make without the proper kitchen equipment and time-consuming under any circumstances, so Bobo recommends using your favorite store-bought frozen french fries—Idaho potatoes will give the best results.

# Pesce Angelica

## Alan Lazarus

| | |
|---|---|
| 1 | tablespoon olive oil |
| 1 | tablespoon chopped green onion |
| 1 or 2 | garlic cloves, pressed |
| ½ | cup sliced canned artichoke hearts |
| ¼ | cup dry white wine |
| 1 | cup whipping cream |
| ½ | cup lump crabmeat (about three to four ounces) |
| 2 | tablespoons Dijon mustard |
| dash | hot pepper sauce or Tabasco |
| 2 | six-ounce fillets of redfish, snapper, or other firm-fleshed white fish |
| ½ | cup all-purpose flour |
| ½ | cup clarified butter |
| | paprika, chopped parsley, lemon, and red caviar for garnish |

Heat the olive oil in large skillet over medium heat. Add the onion and garlic and cook for 2 minutes. Add artichoke hearts and stir for 1 minute. Blend in wine and cook over medium heat until reduced by half. Add cream, and when cream begins to bubble, stir in crabmeat, mustard, and hot pepper sauce. Reduce heat and simmer mixture on very low heat while preparing fish fillets.

Lightly coat the fish fillets with flour on both sides, shaking off any excess. In a second skillet, melt clarified butter over medium-high heat. Add fish and cook until just opaque, turning once (about 2 or 3 minutes per side). Transfer fish to heated plates. Spoon sauce over the fillets. Sprinkle with paprika and chopped parsley. Garnish with half a lemon on the side, with parsley and red caviar on top of the lemon.

*It's best to open a bottle of dry white wine early, because you won't want to take the time to open it once this is ready for the table.*

*Alan and Sherry Lazarus*
*Pesce Angelica with Sauté of Peas,*
*Shitake Mushrooms, and Prosciutto, and wine*

# A LITTLE BIT ON THE SIDE: VEGETABLES, SOUPS, SALADS

Go ahead and admit it. You have always fantasized about slipping in a little bit on the side, especially if you have a motherly instinct. You would like to keep everybody healthy, but frustrating as it may be, they refuse to eat their veggies. Well, try some of these recipes on your hardcore carnivores. Bet you can slip these vegetables in on the side, watch them disappear, and even get some unguarded compliments.

Side dishes can be quite alluring, even if they are not of the two-legged kind. They add color, spice, variety, and a multitude of unexpected flavors. A little bit on the side can be an exciting companion for lonely entrées. But never underestimate the power of a side dish—it could be a meal in itself if you let it.

# Stuffed Zucchini

## Mark Yznaga

| | |
|---|---|
| 2 | medium zucchini |
| 1 | egg |
| 1 | tablespoon milk |
| ¼ | cup chopped cilantro |
| ½ | cup fresh or frozen corn |
| ½ | cup zucchini meat (scooped from the two above) |
| 4 | ounces grated Monterey Jack and cheddar cheese mixed half and half (about ½ cup total) |
| 1 | tablespoon butter |
| | red sauce, salsa fresca, or picante sauce |

Cut the zucchini in half lengthwise and scrape the insides out with a spoon to form "boats" with half-inch-thick sides. Blend the egg, milk, cilantro, corn, zucchini meat, and three fourths of the cheeses (three ounces) in a small bowl. Place the zucchini in a shallow baking dish and fill the cavities with the mixture. Lay thin pats of butter on top and bake in a preheated 325° oven for 45 minutes, or until the zucchini is soft.

Remove from oven, sprinkle the remaining cheese on top, spoon the red sauce, salsa, or picante over the cheese as desired, and bake for another 5 minutes or until the cheese has melted.

Of the three toppings, the red sauce has the mildest flavor but must be prepared. The salsa and picante are spicier and can be purchased ready-made.

### Red sauce

The more adventurous cook, willing to spend an extra half an hour, can make a red sauce with 4 tomatoes, 2 cloves of crushed garlic, 2 tablespoons peanut or corn oil, and a little salt and pepper. Simply immerse the tomatoes in boiling water for about 3 minutes, then peel off the skin and remove the seeds. Sauté the garlic in the oil until golden brown, add the tomatoes, and cook over medium-low heat for 5 minutes. Puree the mixture in the blender and add salt and pepper to taste.

*Mark Yznaga and a friend,*
*Stuffed Zucchini, Stuffed Pimientos,*
*Humus bi Tahini, Souvlaki, and wine*

# Spinach Soufflé

### Horst Pfeifer, Gert Rausch

½ pound fresh spinach
¼ cup whipping cream
2 eggs
pinch nutmeg
pinch salt

Wash, trim, and cook the spinach in boiling water for 2 minutes and drain in a colander. Blend the cooked spinach, cream, and eggs in a food processor or blender. Add nutmeg and salt to taste. Put mixture into buttered egg-poaching cups. Place cups in a baking dish with enough water to come half-way up the side of the cups, and then poach in a preheated oven at 425° for 20 to 25 minutes until thick. They are done when the soufflé is slightly springy to the touch.

# Gratin Dauphinoise

### Horst Pfeifer, Gert Rausch

2 medium potatoes
½ cup whipping cream
½ cup milk
½ teaspoon fresh chopped garlic
pinch nutmeg
pinch salt and pepper

Cook milk with cream, garlic, and seasonings for 2 minutes over medium heat. Peel and slice potatoes very thin (a quarter inch thick) and arrange in a small, one-and-a-half-quart buttered baking dish. Pour liquid over the potatoes and bake in a 425° oven for 20 minutes until done. If the potatoes don't feel crunchy when you stick a sharp knife into them, they are done.

# Poached Pears

### Jeff and Debby Blank

  1     large fresh pear
  2     cups water
  1     cup dry white wine
  ½     cup sugar
  ½     cup lingonberry, currant, or cranberry preserves

Cut the pear in half and remove the core. In a one-quart saucepan, heat the water, sugar, and wine on high until they boil. Add the pear halves and poach on high for 4 minutes. Remove the pear to a serving dish or to dinner plates and fill the cavity with lingonberry (the Scandinavian sister to the cranberry) preserves.

Timing hint: The pears will hold in the poaching water for up to 20 minutes.

# Stir-fry Vegetable Medley

### Jeff and Debby Blank

  1        large carrot
  2        small yellow squash
  1        stalk broccoli
10 to 12   snow peas (optional)
  1        tablespoon butter
  1        clove crushed garlic
  ⅛        teaspoon finely minced fresh ginger
pinch      each of oregano, basil, thyme (fresh if possible)
  2        teaspoons honey or brown sugar
  ¼        cup white wine
           salt and pepper to taste

Clean and slice the vegetables. Combine the remaining ingredients in a sauté pan that has a cover and bring to a simmer over medium heat. Add the sliced vegetables and stir until all are coated with the mixture. Cover and steam in the wine mixture for 2 minutes. Remove the lid and continue to stir until the wine mixture has reduced to two tablespoons or less.

# Bean Sprouts in Soy Sauce

## Marie-Anne and Jean-Louis Dehoux

| | |
|---|---|
| 3 to 4 | ounces chopped bacon (about 4 slices) |
| 1 or 2 | tablespoons water |
| 1 | small yellow onion, chopped |
| 1 | tablespoon soy sauce |
| ¼ | pound fresh bean sprouts |
| | salt and pepper to taste |

In a large saucepan (at least two and a half quarts), "melt" the bacon by cooking it in the water over medium-low heat, until the white, fatty part of the bacon becomes translucent (3 or 4 minutes). Add the onion and continue to cook for another 4 to 5 minutes until the onion begins to soften slightly. Add the bean sprouts and soy sauce and stir thoroughly. Then push the bean sprouts to the edges of the pan, making a hole to the bottom of the pan, and cover. Continue to cook for 7 to 10 more minutes on medium heat.

Making a hole in the center of the ingredients allows the steam to rise and cook the bean sprouts evenly. Be sure that all the water does not boil away; you need the small amount of water in the bottom of the pan to steam the vegetables. Also, be careful not to overcook the bean sprouts. They're ready when they're just past the crisp stage.

This side dish is a delectable complement to the Pork Ardennaise (page 79).

# Mashed Potatoes With Swiss Cheese

## Marie-Anne and Jean-Louis Dehoux

|   |   |
|---|---|
| 2 | small potatoes |
| or 1 | large baking potato |
| 1 | quart water salted to taste |
| 1 | tablespoon butter |
| 1 | egg yolk (optional) |
| ⅛ | teaspoon ground nutmeg |
| ¼ | cup milk or heavy cream |
| ⅓ | cup grated Swiss cheese |
|   | salt and pepper to taste |

Boil the water in a two-quart saucepan. In salting the water remember that the saltiness of the water will equal the saltiness of the potatoes. Peel and dice the potatoes and add them to the water. Cover and cook over medium heat for 10 or 12 minutes until a knife easily pierces the potatoes.

Drain any excess water, add the butter, egg yolk, nutmeg, and half of the milk or cream, and mash with a potato masher until everything is thoroughly mixed. Add more milk or cream as needed to create a medium consistency—not too thick, not too thin, because when you add the cheese, it will have a tendency to thicken. Add the cheese last and mash to mix. Salt and pepper as desired.

# Spanish Rice

## Tony Villegas

| | |
|---|---|
| 1 | cup long-grain rice |
| ¼ | cup oil |
| 1 | large tomato, diced |
| ½ | cup celery, diced |
| ½ | cup bell pepper, diced |
| ½ | onion, diced |
| 1 | tablespoon garlic powder |
| 1 | teaspoon salt |
| 1 | teaspoon comino |
| 1½ | cups water |

In a large skillet over medium-high heat, fry rice in oil for 3 or 4 minutes until slightly brown. Add all of the remaining ingredients and bring to a boil. Reduce heat to medium-low, cover, and cook for 20 to 25 minutes. In the last 10 minutes, remove from heat and allow to stand. The rice will continue to cook from its own heat. When done, all the water will be absorbed by the rice and rice will be tender.

# Avocado Salad

## Tony Villegas

| | |
|---|---|
| 3 | large ripe avocados |
| 1 | large diced tomato |
| ½ | medium onion, chopped |
| 1 | teaspoon garlic powder |
| ½ | lime, juice only |
| 1 | tablespoon vegetable oil |
| | salt to taste |

Pit and peel the avocados, put in a mixing bowl, and smash to a chunky texture. Add the remaining ingredients and mix thoroughly. Chill in the refrigerator until ready to serve. If left to stand too long, cut avocados will turn brown. For the best color and flavor, you should make this salad no more than an hour before you serve it. To choose good avocados, look for the darker purplish color, but not too dark. The overripe ones will be very dark and have a slightly dull finish on the skin. You also want them firm but not too hard, and definitely not soft.

# Cream of Chicken and Wild Rice Soup

## Gary Singer and Lorraine Craft

|       |                                |
|-------|--------------------------------|
| ¼     | cup wild rice and long-grain blend |
| ½     | cup water                      |
| ½     | cup cooked chicken             |
| 2     | tablespoons butter             |
| 2     | tablespoons flour              |
| 1     | chicken bouillon cube          |
| 1     | teaspoon white pepper          |
| ⅛     | teaspoon garlic powder         |
| dash  | onion powder                   |
| ½     | teaspoon chopped parsley       |
| dash  | celery seed                    |
| 1     | cup chicken broth              |
| ½     | cup half-and-half              |

Boil rice in water for 15 minutes and remove from heat. Add all the remaining ingredients, stir together, simmer on low heat for 15 more minutes, and serve. Soup may be thinned with chicken broth or hot milk, if desired.

This soup is a meal in itself when accompanied by steaming hot bread and butter. Dry white wines complement it well.

# Sautéed Mushrooms

## Gary Singer and Lorraine Craft

|     |                                |
|-----|--------------------------------|
| 8   | ounces small mushrooms         |
| 4   | tablespoons lightly salted butter |
| 1   | tablespoon margarine           |
| ½   | teaspoon pure ground pepper    |
| 6   | tablespoons cooking sherry     |

Melt butter and margarine, add pepper, sherry, and mushrooms. Cook over low heat for 10 to 15 minutes until the mushrooms have soaked up the flavors in the pan. Remove from heat and serve immediately.

These mushrooms will add pizzazz to most any beef or chicken dish.

# Chilled Avocado and Crabmeat Soup

## Alan Lazarus

| | |
|---|---|
| 2 | large ripe avocados |
| 2 | cups chicken broth |
| 1 | small clove garlic |
| ½ | teaspoon salt (omit if using canned chicken broth) |
| ¼ | teaspoon white pepper |
| dash | Tabasco |
| | juice of one lime |
| ½ | cup heavy cream |
| ½ | pound fresh lump crabmeat |
| | small package sour cream |
| | red salmon caviar |

Cut avocados in half; remove the pits and peels. Mix avocados, chicken broth, garlic, salt, white pepper, Tabasco, and lime juice in food processor or blender. Pour mixture into a large bowl and stir in the cream and crabmeat.

Chill in the refrigerator for at least 1 hour. Garnish with a sprinkle of shredded crabmeat, a spoonful of sour cream, and a dab of red caviar.

*Alan and Sherry Lazarus*
*Broiled Shrimp with Cashew Pesto,*
*Chilled Avocado and Crabmeat Soup,*
*and white wine*

# Asparagus in Prosciutto

## Mark Holly

| | |
|---|---|
| 8 to 10 | spears fresh asparagus |
| 2 | eighth-inch slices prosciutto (or deli ham) |
| ¼ | cup fresh grated Parmesan |
| ¼ | cup melted butter |
| | fresh ground black pepper |

Preheat oven to 350°. Steam the asparagus for 5 minutes, or until tender. Divide the asparagus into two equal bundles and wrap each bundle with a slice of the meat. Secure with a toothpick if necessary to hold the ham around the asparagus. Place in a shallow baking dish, pour the butter and sprinkle the Parmesan over each bundle, and grind black pepper on top. Bake 8 to 10 minutes or until heated and the cheese is melted.


# Sauté of Peas, Shitake Mushrooms, and Prosciutto

## Alan Lazarus

| | |
|---|---|
| 3 | large fresh shitake mushrooms (use dried if fresh is not available) |
| 1 | tablespoon butter |
| 1 | cup fresh English peas (or frozen baby peas) |
| ¼ | cup diced prosciutto (or smoked ham) |
| 1 | teaspoon minced green onions |
| 1 | tablespoon minced fresh mint |
| | salt and pepper |

If using dried mushrooms, soak them in hot water for 10 to 15 minutes until soft. Squeeze out the excess water and discard any hard stems. Melt butter in a skillet over medium heat. Slice the mushrooms. Combine mushrooms, peas, prosciutto, mint, and green onions in skillet. Stir over medium heat for about 2 minutes until peas are heated through. Season with salt and pepper to taste.

# Sam's Salad

### Sam Irwin

1 medium head of romaine lettuce

**Dressing**

         equal parts virgin olive oil and fresh lemon juice
or 3 tablespoons each virgin olive oil and fresh lemon juice
⅓ cup fresh mint leaves, or a small handful
⅛ teaspoon salt
⅛ teaspoon pepper

Wash the lettuce and break into pieces, drain on a towel or in a colander, and transfer to a large salad bowl. Combine the dressing ingredients, stir, and add additional salt or pepper to taste. Pour dressing over the romaine and toss until all pieces are coated.

Sam says that although this is a typical Lebanese dressing, he likes to consider it his own. It's wonderfully versatile—great before or during a meal, good with meat, fish, or fowl, and very fine with either red or white wine.

# Green Bean Vinaigrette Salad

### Kate Hinds and Dave Meeks

½ pound fresh green beans
1 slice Bermuda onion

**Dressing**

1 tablespoon Dijon mustard
1 tablespoon balsamic vinegar (aged Italian vinegar)
¼ cup virgin olive oil
1 tablespoon chopped parsley

Steam or parboil the beans until tender (about 5 minutes cooking time), then chill and arrange them inside rings of the Bermuda onion. Combine all the dressing ingredients and serve on the side of the plate. (*Shown with Baked Whole Red Snapper on page 80.*)

# Candied Carrots

## Barbara and Bob Asmussen

| | |
|---|---|
| 1 | pound fresh carrots |
| 1 | stick butter |
| ½ | cup brown sugar |
| 1 | teaspoon cinnamon |

In a small saucepan, melt butter and add brown sugar and cinnamon. Cook over low heat for 30 minutes.

Peel and slice fresh carrots. Place in a saucepan with one inch of water and salt if desired, cover, and boil for 5 or 6 minutes. Drain and place in an 8″ × 8″ or other small baking dish. When sauce is ready, pour over carrots and bake in 300° oven for 30 minutes.

An alternate quick method is to add the carrots to the sauce and cook on top of the stove for about 5 minutes, but you'll get a more caramelly carrot if it's baked in the oven.

This sauce is also great on yams.

*It's a promise, these sweet and juicy carrots are just the thing for someone who doesn't like vegetables.*

# Dale's Quick Salad

## Dale Emmert

| | |
|---|---|
| 4 to 6 | leaves of romaine lettuce |
| ¼ | small head of iceberg lettuce |
| 1 | tomato, cut in wedges |
| ½ | Italian bell pepper, cut in ringlets |
| 1 | small avocado, pitted, peeled, and sliced |
| | your favorite Italian or vinaigrette dressing |
| ¼ | cup sesame seeds |

Combine all the vegetables in a medium-size salad bowl and chill in the refrigerator until ready to serve. Then toss with your favorite dressing and sprinkle the sesame seeds over the top.

# Chilled Asparagus With
# French Mustard Vinaigrette

## Chef Emil

| | |
|---|---|
| 16 to 18 | tender spears fresh asparagus |
| | Bibb lettuce leaves |
| | tomato wedges, thinly sliced red onion, and ripe olives for garnish |

### Dressing

| | |
|---|---|
| 1 | teaspoon sugar |
| 1 | teaspoon salt |
| 1 | teaspoon dry mustard |
| 1 | tablespoon cracked black pepper |
| 2 | eggs |
| | juice of one lemon |
| ¼ | cup tarragon wine vinegar |
| 1 | tablespoon Dijon mustard |
| ¼ | cup olive oil |
| 1 | cup vegetable oil |
| ⅛ | cup freshly grated Parmesan cheese |
| 2 | ounces blue cheese |

Combine sugar, salt, dry mustard, and pepper in a mixing bowl. To coddle the eggs, boil one quart of water in a two-quart pan. Add the eggs to the boiling water as you remove it from the burner. Allow the eggs to stand for 4 minutes, then remove them from the hot water immediately. Crack and add the eggs to the mixing bowl. Using a wire whip or electric mixer with a whip attachment (beaters should also work), whip in the lemon juice, vinegar, and Dijon mustard on slow speed until the mixture is well blended. While continuing to whip, combine the oils and slowly pour them into the mixing bowl. This step is similar to making mayonnaise, and the oils must be added slowly to create the proper emulsion and to give the dressing the proper body. When all the oil is added and emulsified, add the Parmesan and blue cheese and whip until the dressing is creamy and well blended.

Trim the asparagus to four inches, cook in boiling water for 3 to 4 minutes until done, drain, and chill. Arrange the asparagus on Bibb lettuce leaves, garnish with tomato wedges, red onions, and olives, and ladle dressing on top.

The dressing is also excellent on artichoke hearts, fresh blanched green beans, or tossed green salads. It should keep well in the refrigerator for up to a week.

# SWEET THINGS:
# DESSERTS

Most desserts are by nature seductive. They cause the salivary glands to go berserk, the *oooo*'s and *aaaahh*'s to begin. You can tell right off how successful you will be by watching the pupils of your lover's eyes when you place the dessert on the table (or where ever). The bigger they get, the more fun you are going to have.

No namby-pamby, light-weight fruits and Jello here. Our motto is: 'Tis better to have eaten dessert and gained, than never to have eaten at all. These sweets are the real thing, from cool chocolate to flaming liqueurs: guaranteed to light your fire and to turn the object of your desire sweet on you.

# Raspberries Flambé
# With Pecan Parfait

*Horst Pfeifer, Gert Rausch*

### The parfait

| | |
|---|---|
| 6 | egg yolks |
| 1 | whole egg |
| 1 | cup powdered sugar |
| 1 | cup roasted pecans (diced) |
| ½ | cup Kahlua |
| 16 | ounces whipped cream |

### The raspberries

| | |
|---|---|
| 2 | tablespoons butter |
| 2 | tablespoons sugar |
| 1 | tablespoon ground orange peel |
| 1 | cup raspberries |
| 2 | ounces 151-proof rum |
| 1 | ounce raspberry liquor or Triple Sec |

The parfait should be prepared the day before. In the top half of a double boiler, whip the egg yolks, egg, and sugar over the steam heat until the mixture thickens. Remove from the heat and allow to cool to room temperature. Add the Kahlua, pecans, and approximately one third of the whipped cream and fold together. Fold in the remaining whipped cream, spoon the mixture into a 9″ × 5″ × 3″ pan, and put in the freezer. Before preparing the raspberries, spoon the parfait into serving glasses or slice it and lay it on a plate with a garnish of fruit and whipped cream.

The raspberries should be prepared just before serving. In a saucepan, melt the butter over medium heat on the stove (or on a Sterno flame at the table if you really want to impress someone). Add all of the remaining ingredients and swirl the pan to mix. Tilt the pan to allow the flame from the Sterno to come into the pan and ignite the alcohol fumes (or you can light the fumes with a match). Cook for 2 to 3 minutes. As the alcohol burns, the flames will subside. You can then spoon the raspberries over the parfait.

*Horst Pfeifer and a friend*
*Pecan Parfait and Raspberries Flambé*

# Bananas Caribe

## Bob Lowe

2    firm but not green bananas
1    stick butter
½    cup dark brown sugar
4    ounces pre-warmed dark rum
1    ounce dark rum
    sour cream for garnish

Peel the bananas and cut along the ridge so that each banana will form two half-moon pieces and lay flat in the pan. Place the banana halves on a plate and set nearby. In a sauté pan over the stove burner or a chafing dish, melt the butter, but be careful not to scorch it. Add the brown sugar and stir to mix it with the butter. Place the bananas in the pan and continue to move them gently so that they will not stick. Keep ladling the sauce over the bananas and keep talking—it makes you seem more casually expert.

When the bananas are a bit more than just warmed through but not cooked soft, introduce the pre-warmed dark rum to the pan. With a small ladle, warm and ignite one ounce of dark rum over a candle flame and add to the pan to ignite the pan. Swirl the pan to excite the flame and keep the bananas from sticking.

Remove the bananas to serving plates. Ladle sauce over the fruit, and stripe the bananas with the sour cream.

# Cherries Jubilee

## *Bob Lowe*

| | |
|---|---|
| 1 | sixteen-ounce can Royal Anne sweet cherries |
| 1 | teaspoon cornstarch |
| 1 to 2 | tablespoons water |
| 2 | ounces Kirsch (cherry brandy) |
| | vanilla ice cream, or light dry cake |

Drain the cherry juice into a sauté pan or chafing dish, and heat over the burner or flame. Dissolve the cornstarch in the water and set nearby. Periodically swirling the pan, cook until the juices begin to thicken. After a few minutes, if the juices do not begin to thicken, add the cornstarch mixture. Continue to cook and thicken the juices for another minute.

Add the cherries and cook until the cherries are heated. Pour the Kirsch in with the cherries. Add an extra splash of Kirsch to a ladle and briefly heat it in the ladle over a candle flame. Ignite the contents of the ladle with the candle flame and pour into the pan to ignite the pan. Agitate the flame by swirling the pan until the flame dies.

Serve immediately over ice cream or cake, or just by itself.

# La Pomme d'Amour
## (The Apple of Love)
### Marie-Anne and Jean-Louis Dehoux

| | |
|---|---|
| 2 | cored and peeled Golden Delicious apples |
| 1 | tablespoon butter |
| 2 | tablespoons sugar |
| dash | cinnamon |
| | |
| 4 | ounces whipping cream |
| 2 | tablespoons sugar |
| 2 | drops water of orange blossom (optional) |
| | |
| 1 | ounce calvados |
| | vanilla ice cream |

Plug the bottom of each cored and peeled apple with half a tablespoon of butter. Place each apple in the center of a 12″ × 12″ sheet of aluminum foil. Fill the cores with one tablespoon each of sugar, and sprinkle cinnamon on top. Pull the edges of the foil straight up over the apple and pinch loosely to the center of the apple. Be sure not to tighten or twist the foil too much. You want to leave a half-inch hole on top to allow steam to escape, but be sure the edges of the foil are completely pulled up to form a bowl. The apples can then be cooked in an oven or on an open fire, such as a barbecue grill, fireplace, or campfire.

## Oven cooked

Preheat oven to 450°, place apples in a baking dish or on a baking sheet, and cook for 25 minutes. To test for doneness, insert a sharp knife, being careful not to pierce the foil. If apple still feels crunchy, cook for another 5 minutes. Jean-Louis tests by pinching the apple with the thumb and forefinger. If the apple feels spongy, it is done. If it resists, it should cook longer.

## Open-flame cooked

Be sure the apples are not in direct contact with the flames. They burn easily. You will have to rely largely on trial and error when using this method; cooking time depends on the placement of the apples in relation to the flames, as well as on the intensity of the fire. Watch the apples closely and check the doneness as you would in the oven-cooked method.

Once the apples are in the oven you can prepare the whipped cream. In a chilled mixing bowl, add the cream, sugar, and water of orange blossom and whip

*Jean-Louis and Marie-Anne Dehoux*
*La Pomme d'Amour, with L'Estro to drink*

with an electric mixer on high speed. (An electric mixer is much easier and faster than whipping by hand with a whisk, but be careful not to overwhip. The cream will "break" into butter and a clear liquid, an irreversible process. It is better to underwhip than to overwhip.) Taste, and add more sugar and flavor as desired. Refrigerate immediately.

Water of orange blossom can be found in most supermarket gourmet sections. It is a very strong orange essence and should be used with caution. It is excellent in pancakes, too.

When done, the apples, still in the foil, should be placed in bowls for support and so they can be handled. Pull the foil away from the apples. Heat the calvados in a metal ladle until almost boiling and flame with a match or by moving the ladle past the open flames. Immediately pour half of the hot calvados on each apple. Add a scoop of vanilla ice cream and a dollop of whipped cream to each apple.

Then try to eat the apple before the ice cream melts.

# Gingerbread With Lemon Sauce
## (Be Ginger With Me Baby)
### Barbara and Bob Asmussen

| | |
|---|---|
| ½ | cup Crisco |
| 1 | cup sugar |
| 3 | eggs |
| 1 | cup sour milk |
| 2½ | cups flour |
| 1 | cup molasses |
| 1 | teaspoon ginger |
| 1 | teaspoon cinnamon |
| 2 | teaspoons baking soda |

### Lemon Sauce

| | |
|---|---|
| ½ | cup sugar |
| 1 | tablespoon cornstarch |
| 1 | teaspoon grated lemon rind |
| ¼ | teaspoon salt |
| 1 | cup boiling water |
| 2 | tablespoons butter |
| 4 | tablespoons lemon juice |

To make gingerbread, cream the Crisco, sugar, and eggs in a mixing bowl with an electric mixer. Add the remaining ingredients and blend thoroughly until creamy. Pour into a greased and floured 9″×9″ baking pan. Bake at 325° for 40 to 45 minutes, or until the sides of the gingerbread begin to pull away from the pan.

To make lemon sauce, combine sugar, cornstarch, lemon rind, salt, and water in a saucepan. Cook over medium-high heat until the mixture becomes clear. Add the lemon juice and butter, stirring until butter is melted and thoroughly blended. Pour the lemon sauce over pieces of gingerbread, and serve while still warm.

*One bite of this will make your adored pucker up for a big ginger kiss.*

# Baked Apples and Hot Rum Sauce
## (Adam's Downfall)
### Barbara and Bob Asmussen

|  |  |
|---|---|
| 2 | cored, unpeeled apples |

**Pastry**

|  |  |
|---|---|
| 1⅓ | cups flour |
| ½ | teaspoon salt |
| ½ | cup Crisco |
| 3 or 4 | tablespoons cold water |

**Rum sauce**

|  |  |
|---|---|
| 1 | stick of butter |
| 1 | cup honey |
| ¼ | cup brown sugar |
| 3 | tablespoons rum flavoring |

In a mixing bowl, combine flour and salt. Add Crisco and cut, or blend, with a fork. Add water and thoroughly mix. Divide into Ping-Pong-size balls and roll out on floured surface. The dough should be rolled out to five or six inches in diameter. Place an apple in center of pastry and fold pastry over the apple, tucking the edges into the center of the apple. If you're feeling artistic, use the extra pastry to mold leaves and stems. Put the apples in a deep baking pan. Bake 1½ hours at 350°, or until golden brown.

To make rum sauce, melt butter in saucepan. Add the remaining ingredients and cook over low heat for 20 minutes. Do not boil. Pour over hot baked apples.

Serve the apples while still hot. Add a scoop of ice cream, and you can present your love with an irresistible temptation.

# Blackberry Cobbler
### (Berry, Berry Good)
**Barbara and Bob Asmussen**

### Filling

| | |
|---|---|
| 1 | pound fresh or defrosted frozen blackberries |
| 1½ | cups sugar |
| 2 | tablespoons lemon juice |
| 1 | tablespoon flour |
| dash | salt |
| 2½ | cups water |

### Pastry

| | |
|---|---|
| 2 | cups flour |
| ½ | teaspoon salt |
| ¾ | cup Crisco |
| 6 to 8 | tablespoons cold water |

Combine all the filling ingredients except the water and mix thoroughly. Add water, stir, and set aside.

To make the pastry, combine salt with flour. Add Crisco and cut into the flour. Add six tablespoons of water and mix thoroughly. Add extra water only if needed. Roll out the dough on a floured surface, keeping as thin as possible. Cut one-inch-wide strips of dough to weave a top crust, using end pieces and extras to cut into one-inch-square dumplings.

Add dumplings to berries and mix. Pour into a 9″ × 13″ baking dish. Arrange the pastry strips on top to form a woven crust. Bake at 350° for 1½ hours, or until crust is golden brown.

Serve while hot with ice cream. This cobbler should bedazzle your love, especially if you follow it with a fruit liqueur.

# My Favorite Dessert
### (A Sweet Affair)
### Dale Emmert

**For two**

| | |
|---|---|
| 1 | pint fresh strawberries with green stems |
| ¾ | pound assorted Belgian gourmet milk chocolates |
| 8 | beignets |
| ½ | cup sifted powdered sugar |
| ¾ | cup of your favorite chocolate sauce |

**For six or more**

| | |
|---|---|
| 2 | pints fresh strawberries with green stems |
| 2 | pounds assorted Belgian gourmet milk chocolates |
| 2 | dozen beignets |
| 1 | cup sifted powdered sugar |
| 2 | cups of your favorite chocolate sauce |

In two medium or one large brandy snifter, arrange a layer of strawberries stems up. (For the recipe for six or more, use an eight-inch-diameter clear truffle dish.) In a separate pan, sprinkle beignets with the powdered sugar, then spread a layer of them on top of the strawberries in the snifter or truffle dish. Then arrange the chocolates in a third layer on top of the beignets. Repeat a layer of each so you have a total of six alternating layers. The arrangement is limited only by your imagination. Use different serving dishes, or try placing a flower on top.

Pour the chocolate sauce into an attractive serving dish and place on the table with the dessert and a serving spoon. (You can also reserve half of the milk chocolates, melt them in a double boiler, and serve in a mini-chafing dish with a votive warmer.) The fresh strawberries and beignets should be dipped in the chocolate sauce and popped into the mouth.

This dish *must* be served with champagne. Tall glasses, soft music, a fire in the fireplace, and perhaps a game of Trivial Pursuit or Scrabble are Dale and Debra's suggestions for turning your evening into a sweet affair.

Dale and Debra Emmert
*My Favorite Dessert and champagne*

# Rum Balls

## Gary Singer and Lorraine Craft

¾    cup finely grated vanilla wafers
⅓    cup crushed pecans
2    teaspoons cocoa
2    teaspoons white corn syrup
1    ounce brandy, rum, or Cointreau

### Coating

¼    cup cocoa
¼    cup powdered sugar

Combine all ingredients in a medium mixing bowl and thoroughly mix. Shape by teaspoonfuls into balls. Mix equal parts of cocoa and powdered sugar, and roll the balls in the mixture to coat. Makes twelve rum balls that will disappear quickly.

# Frozen Margarita Pie

## Tony Villegas

1    ten-inch graham cracker pie shell
1    sixteen-ounce can sweetened condensed milk
¼    cup fresh lime juice
4    tablespoons tequila
4    tablespoons Triple Sec
2    cups whipping cream (16 ounces or 1 pint)

This dessert should be prepared the day before.

Combine the milk, lime juice, tequila, and Triple Sec in a large bowl and beat with an electric mixer on high speed for about 4 minutes until smooth. The mixture will begin to thicken. Add the whipping cream to the mixture and beat 2 minutes until thoroughly mixed. The filling will thicken more and take on body. Pour mixture into pie shell and freeze overnight. Put into the refrigerator 1 hour before serving. Garnish the top with whipped cream and strawberries.

A whole pie is certainly more than enough for two people, and leftovers can simply be refrozen.

# Sweet Susan

### Sam Irwin

2 cups fresh raspberries
½ cup Grand Marnier

chocolate chip ice cream

In a ten-inch sauté pan or skillet, over medium heat, simmer raspberries with Grand Marnier for 3 or 4 minutes and spoon over hard frozen chocolate chip ice cream.

To make this even more seductive, chill the bowls, garnish with a sprig of mint, and offer with a snifter of brandy and coffee.

# Chocolate Mousse

### Bobo Van Mechelen

4 ounces bittersweet chocolate, preferably
gourmet Swiss
2 tablespoons milk
2 tablespoons sugar
4 eggs, separated

Break up the chocolate into a saucepan and add the milk and sugar. Over very low heat, warm the mixture until the chocolate and sugar are melted. Add the egg yolks and thoroughly stir into the chocolate mixture, remove from the heat, and let stand for 15 minutes.

In a large mixing bowl, whip the egg whites until stiff. Add the chocolate mixture and stir slowly, folding the egg whites and chocolate together until mixed. Pour into dessert glasses and chill in the refrigerator at least 2 hours.

Garnish with whipped cream, and serve with coffee. Afterwards, for the final European touch, offer your love a cognac.

# SPLENDOR IN THE GLASS: DRINKS

Drink is a necessity of life. Some think that drinking something with a little alcohol in it is also a necessity. Most of the chefs recommend moderation with all of the following drink recipes. For one thing, in large quantities they can give you that bloated feeling or otherwise take the starch out of your sex life. Take it from Shakespeare, drinking "provokes the desire, but it takes away the performance."

But if you are one of those people who believe that anything worth doing is worth doing to excess, arrange to indulge your excesses at home—or at the home of someone who doesn't mind spending the night with you, no matter what state you're in or whose lampshade you've been dancing with.

*Sam Irwin and a friend*
*Moscow Mules and Prairie Fires*

# Moscow Mule

## Sam Irwin

1½     **ounces premium vodka**
       **ginger beer**
       **lime wedges**

Ideally, a Moscow Mule should be served in a copper cup, but if you don't have any available, glass mugs or highball glasses will do.

Fill the cup or glass with ice. Add the vodka, then fill the glass with ginger beer. Give it a quick stir if you like (although the bubbles in the ginger beer have a tendency to do the stirring for you), and add a squeeze of lime and a lime wedge.

*The appropriate toast with this is "Broscht," as they say in Moscow. But watch out. These are so good you'll be tempted to have more than one, and too many may make you as hardheaded as a mule.*

# Prairie Fire

## Sam Irwin

       **juice of one lime**
1     **squirt Rose's lime juice (about 1 teaspoon)**
2     **dashes of Tabasco sauce (more if you like it hot)**
2½     **ounces Cuervo Gold tequila**

Start with a shaker of ice. Add all of the above ingredients, shake well (be sure to shake the drink too), and pour through a strainer into two 2-ounce shot glasses.

# Mimosa

### Jeff and Debby Blank

| | |
|---|---|
| 4 | ounces chilled, fresh-squeezed orange juice |
| 4 | ounces chilled champagne |
| 1 | ounce Triple Sec or other orange liqueur |
| | orange wheel and mint for garnish |

The night before, chill the champagne flutes in the freezer and the champagne and orange juice in the refrigerator. Combine the above ingredients in a shaker with ice and stir lightly until mixed, pour through a strainer into the chilled champagne flutes, and serve with garnishes.

Sunday brunch is not complete without this light, bubbly, and simple drink. Like any champagne drink, the Mimosa should be icy cold. Any drinking glass will do, but the champagne flute shows off the bubbles and holds the effervescence longer.

# Sangria

### Debby Blank

| | |
|---|---|
| 1 | liter of red Bordeaux |
| ¼ | cup Cointreau |
| ¼ | cup brandy |
| ¼ | cup orange juice |
| ¼ | cup lemon juice |
| 3 | tablespoons sugar |
| 1 | sliced orange, lime, and lemon |
| ½ | pint fresh strawberries, sliced |

Combine all of the ingredients in a pitcher and pour into glasses of ice. Garnish the rim of the glasses with wheels of any of the fruits.

# Ramos Gin Fizz

## Mark Holly

2 ounces gin
1 ounce Triple Sec
½ ounce lime juice
½ ounce lemon juice
4 ounces half-and-half
2 teaspoons sugar
4 drops vanilla
1 egg white
  lime slices for garnish

Combine all of the above ingredients in a shaker with ice, shake well, and strain into two 4-ounce glasses. Garnish with a lime wheel.

*A gin fizz will add sparkle to a breakfast, brunch, or evening appetizer.*


# Champagne Cocktail

## Mark Holly

2 sugar cubes
2 dashes angostura bitters
  chilled champagne

Put a sugar cube in each champagne glass and pour several drops of the bitters on each cube. Pour the chilled champagne over the sugar cubes and serve immediately.

*The champagne cocktail, with its bittersweet twist, is certainly appropriate for any occasion.*

# L'Estro

## (A State of Mind)
### Marie-Anne and Jean-Louis Dehoux

5   ounces orange juice
1   ounce cognac
1   ounce Cointreau or Triple Sec

Wet the rims of two tall champagne glasses and dip in sugar, leaving a half-inch ring of sugar on the rims.

In a shaker, combine all the drink ingredients, shake with ice, and strain into the two champagne glasses. Serve with a quarter slice of orange on the rim of the glass if desired.

# Café de Leon

## Mark Holly

### Makes one drink:

¾   jigger Kahlua (1½ ounces)
½   jigger amaretto (1 ounce)
¼   jigger Grand Marnier (½ ounce)
1   stick cinnamon
1   ounce half-and-half
    brewed coffee
    whipped cream (optional)

Combine the Kahlua, amaretto, Grand Marnier, cinnamon stick, and half-and-half in a coffee mug or heavy glass. Fill the remainder of the mug or glass with coffee and top with whipped cream if desired.

*Café de Leon can be a dessert all by itself. It's the perfect drink to sip on during your late-night snuggling up.*

# Bloody Mary

## Gary Singer and Lorraine Craft

¼ teaspoon ground pepper
¼ teaspoon celery salt
⅛ teaspoon salt
1 tablespoon Worcestershire sauce
1 tablespoon lemon juice
12 ounces tomato juice
2 ounces vodka

lime wedges and celery stalks for garnish

Combine all the drink ingredients in a shaker and mix well. Pour into two glasses over ice. Garnish with a lime wedge and a stalk of celery.

*The Bloody Mary is one of the most popular breakfast drinks, but it also goes well with many appetizers and of course is great just for sipping.*


# Margarita

## Tony Villegas

2 ounces Triple Sec
3 ounces tequila
2 ounces lime juice
2 ounces water (omit if making frozen
   ones in the blender)
2 teaspoons sugar
   salt and lime for garnish

Salt the rims of two glasses by wetting them with lime juice and dipping the glasses into salt. This, of course, is optional if you are trying to avoid salt. Combine all of the ingredients in a shaker, shake well, and pour over ice into the glasses. Garnish with a lime wheel or lime wedge on the rim.

# Raspberry Champagne

### Horst Pfeifer, Gert Rausch

| | |
|---|---|
| 1½ | cups raspberries |
| | juice of one lemon |
| 1 | teaspoon sugar |
| 1 | bottle well-chilled champagne |

Combine the raspberries, lemon juice, and sugar in a food processor or blender and puree. Strain the mixture through a wire mesh strainer to remove any seeds. Fill two chilled champagne flutes one fourth of the way full with the raspberry mixture. Fill the remainder of the glass with chilled champagne.

For a refreshing variation, try other fruits in season.

# Café Brûlot

### Bob Lowe

| | |
|---|---|
| 4 | ounces cognac or good brandy |
| splash | Cointreau |
| | zest of one orange quarter |
| | zest of one lemon quarter |
| 2 | whole cloves |
| 1 | small cinnamon stick |
| pinch | vanilla bean (optional) |
| 2 | cups strong coffee |
| | small lumps of sugar |

In a saucepan, combine and heat all of the ingredients except the coffee. Warm a serving bowl (a silver Revere bowl works well) and pour the heated liquors into it. Pick up a bit of the liquor in a small ladle and ignite by touching to a candle flame. (Matches are gauche.) Add the ladleful of flaming liquor to the bowl to flame the bowl. Gently toss the liquid with the ladle to excite the flame while pouring coffee down the side of the bowl to flow under the liquor. When the flame burns out, serve in a demitasse with a small lump of sugar.

# FOOD FORE PLAY:
# SNACKS

Every once in a while you've just got to let yourself go. You can go nuts, salted or unsalted. You can go bananas, with whipped cream and cherries, or ice cream on top—or nothing on at all. Get that chip off your shoulder and into the dip, or you can just go crackers. Whether it's midnight or midmorning, there is a perfect snack for you to fool around with.

Junk food can have an important place in a romance. A craving for onion rings is the sort of thing that can bring people together, and hogging the green M&M's is the sort of thing that can tear a relationship apart. The sexiest foods, though, are the ones that give you a sense of forbidden indulgence, of getting away with something that you shouldn't. And that's what these recipes are for: intimate, outrageous pleasures.

*Horst Pfeifer and a friend*
*Teasing Delicacies and Raspberry Champagne*

# Teasing Delicacies

## Horst Pfeifer, Gert Rausch

|          |                                                        |
|----------|--------------------------------------------------------|
| 1        | loaf fresh French bread, cut in quarter-inch slices    |
| 1 or 2   | tablespoons butter                                     |
| 5        | ounces fresh salmon meat, ground juice of half a lime  |
| 1        | tablespoon olive oil                                   |
| pinch    | dill, salt, and pepper                                 |
| 2        | thin slices roast beef                                 |
| 1        | ounce cream cheese                                     |
| 6 to 8   | small, cooked asparagus tips                           |
| 2        | thin slices pâté of your choice                        |
| 2        | thin slices Brie cheese                                |
| 2        | thin slices smoked salmon or lox fresh ground horseradish sauce |

At least two hours before assembling the delicacy tray, blend the fresh ground salmon meat with the lime juice, olive oil, dill, and salt and pepper. Refrigerate, stirring occasionally. (This is a salmon tartare and is to remain uncooked.) Next, spread each of the roast beef slices with half an ounce of cream cheese, then roll each one around three or four asparagus tips and refrigerate.

Just before you assemble the delicacy tray, toast the slices of French bread and pat with butter to form bite-size toast points.

On each toast point, place one of the following: salmon spread, roast beef, pâté, Brie, or smoked salmon with horseradish sauce. Arrange the toast points on a tray and serve with your choice of fresh fruits or vegetables, such as black or green grapes, cherries, kiwi fruit, peaches, sliced carrots, celery, cucumber with lemon wedges.

These delicacies are excellent with Raspberry Champagne (page 125).

# Pico de Gallo
## (Really Hot Stuff)
### Michael Young

| | |
|---|---|
| 1 | medium onion, diced |
| 1 | medium ripe tomato, diced |
| 2 | serrano chiles, seeded and finely chopped |
| 2 | sprigs cilantro, chopped |
| 1 | tablespoon oil and vinegar dressing |
| | juice of half a lime |
| | salt and pepper to taste |
| 1 or 2 | avocados |

Combine all ingredients except avocados and chill for half an hour. When ready to serve, cube the avocados and gently fold into chilled mixture. Try to keep the avocado pieces as intact as possible. The avocado should be chunky, not mashed.

Serve with warm tostada chips and a cold beer or margarita, or as a side dish with fajitas or tacos.

*Mike likes to have Pico de Gallo while overlooking Acapulco Bay. He says it's worth the trip, but if you can't make it, any patio, balcony, or poolside will certainly do.*

# Spanakopita Triangles

## Mark Yznaga

| | |
|---|---|
| 4 | large sheets fillo dough |
| ½ | cup melted butter |

### Filling

| | |
|---|---|
| ¼ | pound crumbled feta cheese |
| ¼ | pound large-curd cottage cheese |
| 1 | egg |
| ¼ | teaspoon oregano |
| ¼ | teaspoon nutmeg |
| pinch | cloves |
| pinch | black pepper |
| 1 | small green onion finely chopped (about 2 tablespoons) |
| 1 | tablespoon chopped parsley |

Fillo is a very thin dough that comes stacked in sheets like tissue paper and is then folded and packaged to preserve the freshness. It can be purchased in specialty food and gourmet shops. It is the dough out of which croissants are made.

To prepare the filling, simply combine all of the filling ingredients in the blender and blend until thoroughly mixed. Do not overblend.

Lay a sheet of fillo on a flat surface (a large cutting board), brush the melted butter over the top side of the sheet, and cut lengthwise into three-inch strips. At the bottom of each strip, place a teaspoonful of filling. Fold the bottom edge around the filling diagonally, and continue to fold as you would a flag. When you have folded to the end of the strip (it will form a triangle), seal the edges with butter. Brush both sides of each triangle with butter. Place on a cookie sheet with some space between each triangle and bake in a preheated 325° oven for 10 minutes or until golden.

Every oven, whether gas or electric, has its temperature idiosyncrasies, so check the Spanakopitas after about five minutes. If they are turning brown on the edges too quickly, turn the temperature down 25°. You want an even, deep golden color when done.

*Mark Yznaga and a friend*
*Spanakopita and red wine*

# Potted Smoked Salmon

### Kate Hinds and Dave Meeks

8     ounces softened cream cheese
2     tablespoons softened butter
4     ounces smoked salmon
      juice of half a lemon

Blend cream cheese and butter in food processor or blender. Remove skin and any bones from salmon. Crumble and add to cream cheese mixture with lemon juice. Blend just enough to distribute the salmon in the cheese. Do not overblend.

Pack the mixture into a small crock and serve with French bread slices or cocktail rye bread, sliced red onion, capers, and a sprinkling of fresh dill. And, of course, champagne.

# Smoked Alaskan Salmon With Capers and Bermuda Onions

### Dale Emmert

smoked Alaskan salmon, sliced very thin
cream cheese
capers
chopped Bermuda onion
chopped boiled eggs
French bread

Dale doesn't list quantities in this recipe because it can double as a snack or a full meal. His recommendation is to let your appetite be your guide. Try this with a dry California or French champagne or a French Chablis.

# Richboy Sandwich

## Bob Lowe

1      bottle well-chilled brut champagne

8      ounces fresh oysters

¼      cup butter

2      hoagie rolls

Drain the oysters. In a chafing dish over a Richaud stove (if you have one) or in a sauté pan over the range (but it's not as glamorous), melt the butter, being careful not to brown it. Turn the oysters into the butter, and turn them with a spoon until the edges begin to curl. Pour in about one eighth of the champagne. It will sizzle, and the aroma will knock you out! Keep turning the oysters and the sauce until bubbling well. (The oysters do not have to be cooked, but the bath in champagne is very important.)

Split the hoagie rolls and lightly toast over an open flame. Butterfly the rolls on plates, and lay oysters over the open face of the rolls. Lightly reduce the sauce for another minute or two in the pan, pour over the oysters and rolls, and serve immediately as the two of you sip on the remaining ice-cold champagne.

*What a marvelous midnight snack!*

# Green Chile and Cream Cheese Dip

## Barbara and Bob Asmussen

1      eight-ounce package cream cheese

1      four-ounce can diced green chiles

½      cup sour cream

dash      garlic salt

Put all of the ingredients in the blender. Then blend!

Go ahead and make plenty of this to have on hand. It just gets better with age. Serve with crackers or chips.

# Free Toes

## (It's a 10)

### Anonymous


| 1 | bag of corn chips |
| ½ | pint of your favorite dip |
| 2 | pedicures (optional) |

Place your lover's foot on a serving tray. Open the corn chips and place a chip between each toe on the foot, then pile the rest of the chips around the foot. Dab a little dip on each toe, and serve on a red heart-shaped pillow with beer, your favorite cola, or anything you think can stand up to corn chips.

This dish requires a lot of concentration—once you start giggling, it's guaranteed to raise your arches.


# Cracker Jazz-up

## (Poppin' Good)

### Anonymous


| ¼ | cup unpopped popcorn |
| 4 | tablespoons butter |
| ½ | cup milk |
| 1 | cup sugar |

Pop the popcorn the way you like it, then set aside in a large bowl.

Melt butter in large skillet. Add milk and sugar. Stir continuously over high heat. Mixture will swell up and rise substantially. Continue stirring until mixture takes on a light brown color, resembling light brown sugar, then pour over popcorn. Mix with popcorn immediately to coat all kernels.

Allow to cool for 5 minutes before eating, or you'll burn your tongue. Hotcha!

# GARNISH YOUR LOVE

Sight is usually the first sense to be stimulated by a handsome man or a beautiful woman—or a delectable plate of food. Any dish, human or culinary, will get a better reception if it is dolled up a bit. Presentation and service are the most effective aphrodisiacs known to man and woman. On a scale of one to ten, garnishes can take a meal that's a seven and pump it up to a nine and a half. And most of them are easy and inexpensive.

Garnishes should be made from fresh, edible items, such as fruits, olives, vegetables, and fresh herbs. If you keep one or two items handy from each of the following categories, you'll be ready to add the final touches to almost any romantic meal.

### Fresh fruits

| | | |
|---|---|---|
| apples (all colors) | limes | kiwis |
| strawberries | oranges | grapes (all kinds) |
| nectarines | cherries | watermelons |
| honeydew melons | cantaloupes | plums |
| peaches | pineapples | lemons |
| limes | bananas | |

### Vegetables

| | | |
|---|---|---|
| lettuce (all types) | red cabbage | avocados |
| onions | shallots | bell peppers |
| Italian bell peppers | tomatoes | Bermuda onions |
| celery | carrots | cherry tomatoes |
| watercress | radishes | |

### Herbs, olives, miscellaneous

| | |
|---|---|
| fresh parsley | green olives |
| black olives | fresh mushrooms |
| fresh cilantro | caviar |
| Greek olives | eggs |

It's best to keep it simple, to use one or two items at a time. The idea is to add color and shapes to a plate as you do when you put on a necktie or earrings.

*Bon appétit* **and** *bon amour!*

# THE CHEFS
## Their Restaurants and Their Recipes

### Barbara and Bob Asmussen

**Barbara Ellen's Hill Country Restaurant**
**13129 Highway 71 West**
**Bee Cave, Texas 78746**
**(512) 263-2385**

*Fajitas*
*Meat Loaf*
*Stuffed Artichokes*
*Pork With Jezebel Sauce*
*Candied Carrots*
*Gingerbread With Lemon Sauce*
*Blackberry Cobbler*
*Baked Apples and Hot Rum Sauce*
*Green Chili Cream Cheese Dip*

### Jeff and Debby Blank

**Hudson's-on-the-Bend**
**3509 F.M. 620 North**
**Austin, Texas 78734**
**(512) 266-1369**

*Hill Country Breakfast*
*Chilled Smoked Shrimp and Orange Ginger*
*    Barbecue Sauce*
*Mesquite-Grilled Venison Tenderloin*
*Poached Pears*
*Stir-fry Vegetable Medley*
*Mimosa*
*Sangria*

### Marie-Anne and Jean-Louis Dehoux

**The Belgian Restaurant L'Estro Armonico**
**3520 Bee Cave Road**
**Austin, Texas 78746**
**(512) 328-0580**

*Croissants and Coffee*
*Pork Ardennaise*
*Bean Sprouts in Soy Sauce*
*Mashed Potatoes With Swiss Cheese*
*La Pomme d'Amour*
*L'Estro, "A State of Mind"*

### Dale Emmert

**The Capitol Oyster Company**
**219 West Fifteenth Street**
**Austin, Texas 78701**
**(512) 478-8377**
**and Capitol Cuisines**
**One Capitol Square**
**300 West Fifteenth Street, Suite 101**
**Austin, Texas 78701**

*Shrimp Remoulade*
*Bourbon Street Chicken*
*Dale's Quick Salad*
*My Favorite Dessert*
*Smoked Alaskan Salmon With Capers*
*    and Bermuda Onions*

**Kate Hinds and Dave Meeks**

Kate's
509 Hearn Avenue
Austin, Texas 78703
(512) 477-6535

Grilled Tuna Niçoise Salad
Oysters With Horseradish
Baked Whole Red Snapper With Saffron
Veal Rolled With Fontina Cheese
    and Prosciutto
Green Bean Vinaigrette Salad
Potted Smoked Salmon


**Chef Mark Holly**

The Jambalaya Restaurant
6801 Burnet Road
Austin, Texas 78757
(512) 453-8574

Hidden Treasure
Crab-Stuffed Avocado
Shrimp-Stuffed Mushrooms
Asparagus in Prosciutto
Ramos Gin Fizz
Champagne Cocktail
Café de Leon


**Sam Irwin**

Birraporetti's
905 Barton Springs Road
Austin, Texas 78704
(512) 480-8446

Golden Rod
Sam's Salad
Sweet Susan
Moscow Mule
Prairie Fire


**Alan Lazarus**

Basil's
900 West Tenth Street
Austin, Texas 78703
(512) 477-5576

Broiled Shrimp With Cashew Pesto
Pesce Angelica
Sauté of Peas, Shitake Mushrooms,
    and Prosciutto
Chilled Avocado and Crabmeat Soup


**Bob Lowe**

Galleria
One Jefferson Square
Austin, Texas 78703
(512) 452-5510

Bananas Caribe
Cherries Jubilee
Café Brûlot
Richboy Sandwich

### Chef Horst Pfeifer and Gert Rausch

Austin's Courtyard
1205 North Lamar Boulevard
Austin, Texas 78703
(512) 476-7095

Mixed Caesar Salad With Seafood
Quail Galantine With Orange Sauce
and Pink Peppercorns
Lobster-Stuffed Lamb Chop in Pastry
With Red Buttersauce
Spinach Soufflé
Gratin Dauphinoise
Raspberries Flambé With Pecan Parfait
Raspberry Champagne
Teasing Delicacies

### Gary Singer and Lorraine Craft

Dan McKlusky's Restaurant
419 East Sixth Street
Austin, Texas 78701
(512) 473-8924
and 10000-A Research Boulevard
Austin, Texas 78759
(512) 346-0780

Eggs Napoleon
Chicken Parmesan
Sautéed Mushrooms
Cream of Chicken and Wild Rice Soup
Rum Balls
Bloody Mary

### Chef Raymond Tatum

Jeffrey's
1204 West Lynn Street
Austin, Texas 78703
(512) 477-5584

Oriental Grilled Pork Chops
Redfish in Lemon Butter
Chicken Breasts in Mushroom Red Wine
Sauce
Lamb Chops With Green Peppercorn Butter

### Bobo Van Mechelen

Gambrinus Belgian Bar & Restaurant
314 Congress Avenue
Austin, Texas 78701
(512) 472-0112

Soft-boiled Eggs With Toast Fingers
Steak Tartare
Steak au Poivre à la Crème
Lobster With Special Red Sauce
and Homemade Mayonnaise
Chocolate Mousse

### Tony Villegas

El Mercado Restaurant
1302 South First Street
Austin, Texas 78704
(512) 447-7445

Migas (With Tortilla Squares) and Home Fries
Carne Asada Fresca
Shrimp Ceviche Salad
Spanish Rice
Avocado Salad
Frozen Margarita Pie
Margarita

*Chef Emil Vogely*  *Pain Perdu*
*Stuffed Quail (Smoked)*
*Stuffed Summer Squash*
*Truche de Amor*
*Chilled Asparagus With French Mustard*
  *Vinaigrette*


**Michael Young**  *Migas (With Chips)*
*Fettuccine Alfredo*
**Chuy's Comida Deluxe**  *Ceviche*
**1728 Barton Springs Road**  *Pico de Gallo*
**Austin, Texas 78704**
**(512) 474-4452**


*Mark Yznaga*  *Souvlaki, Cypriot Style*
*Stuffed Roasted Pimientos*
**The Common Market**  *Humus bi Tahini*
**1610 San Antonio**  *Stuffed Zucchini*
**Austin, Texas 78701**  *Spanakopita Triangles*
**(512) 472-1900**

# Index